Exotic Territory:
A Bilingual Anthology of Contemporary Paraguayan Poetry

Also by Ronald Haladyna

La contextualización de la poesía postmoderna mexicana

Rescatando la poesía paraguaya: Diez ensayos sobre nueve poetas

Contemporary Uruguayan Poetry: A Bilingual Anthology

Exotic Territory: A Bilingual Anthology of Contemporary Paraguayan Poetry

Edited by Ronald Haladyna

Introduction, Translations, Bibliographies, and Notes by the Editor

Order this book online at www.trafford.com
or email orders@trafford.com

Most Trafford titles are also available at major online book retailers.

Printed in the United States of America.

ISBN: 978-1-4269-6696-5 (sc)
ISBN: 978-1-4269-6697-2 (hc)
ISBN: 978-1-4269-6699-6 (e)

Library of Congress Control Number: 2011907037

Trafford rev. 05/23/2011

www.trafford.com

North America & international
toll-free: 1 888 232 4444 (USA & Canada)
phone: 250 383 6864 • fax: 812 355 4082

To Sergio,
whose love for Paraguay equals mine

Contents

Preface

The intention of this anthology is to introduce to the English-reading world contemporary poetry of Paraguay, a remote, exotic, and little-known land in the middle of South America. In the past forty years, Latin America has achieved universal recognition for its narrative literature, but that has not been the case for its poetry. Although Nobel Prize winners Pablo Neruda (1971) and Octavio Paz (1990) aroused some recognition of Latin American poetry, only a few other current poets—perhaps Nicanor Parra, Juan Gelman, Ernesto Cardenal, Sub Commander Marcos—are recognized in North American literary and university circles, or by literary researchers. The current *MLA International Bibliography* references only a handful of articles on current Latin American poets.

It may seem strange that most South American poets are unfamiliar with celebrated poets of their neighboring countries. What is not so strange is that the general reading public in North America is not only unfamiliar with South America's poetry, but also with its history, geography, economy, politics, and culture. This bilingual anthology is an attempt to give long-overdue recognition to Paraguay's leading contemporary poets.

The selection of poets and poetry representing an entire nation is always problematic at best, and at worst susceptible to suspicions of ignorance or partiality, based on dubious inclusions or unpardonable omissions. Anthologists, just like poets, are subjective creatures, relying on personal reading experience, acquired tastes, a thirst for novelty, and even raw instinct. Beyond these considerations, the conscientious anthologist is obliged to take into consideration some broadly based and reasonable literary criteria for selection, including any of the following: a poetic sensibility, manifested through thought-provoking themes and ideas; a special perspective of reality, be it personal, local, national or universal; a unique style; and a convincing command of language. In addition, I look for mature, dedicated poets with a sustained, recognized publication history of books of poetry, (in this case I have chosen the last two decades); and some evidence of peer recognition mostly through published reviews and interviews, but also prologues and essays. This last criterion often falls by the wayside in countries such as Paraguay, where poetry is only occasionally and superficially reviewed in local media and rarely is the focus of scholarly analysis. I have also been swayed by poets who have received literary awards both at home and abroad and whose poems have been included in national and international Spanish-language anthologies and literary reviews.

For the purposes of selection for this anthology, my intention has been to introduce outstanding and representative contemporary Paraguayan poets from the last several decades and to translate representative poems for readers unfamiliar with Spanish. I have attempted here to gather an array of poets representing different "generations"—some in fact have been published since the 1940s—who have been actively writing and publishing books of significant quality and quantity to represent the genre convincingly. Also, I have wished to present the great diversity extant in stylistic approaches, perspectives, imagination, ideas, and language in Paraguay's recent poetry.

This anthology has been long in the making; it started with a Fulbright teaching/research award I received in 1997 with which I taught a course on postmodern poetry at the Universidad Católica in Asunción. The research part of the Fulbright experience consisted of extensive reading of scores of contemporary Paraguayan poets (in Spanish, not in Guaraní), condensing a list of what I considered to be the most significant, representative and interesting poets, and then selecting a variety of poems of each one. I also carried out a series of interviews to capture the poets' sense of their own poetics, as well as to explore their perspectives on possible societal and literary influences on their works to aid me in my translations.

For virtually all of the bibliographies of primary and secondary sources of these poets, I started from scratch. None of the poets had a complete bibliography of their own published works, let alone of published reviews, interviews, and criticism on their works. I have included bio-bibliographies as an initial guide for future research. Given the lack of resources in Paraguay, it was difficult to get an exhaustive listing of secondary sources and complete bibliographical data, but this data will provide a base for future researchers to build upon. Nobody has ever proposed a canon of contemporary Paraguayan poets, but I hope this project will provide a meaningful step toward opening such a discussion.

TRANSLATION NOTES

The cultural flavor, the idiomatic nuances, the flexibility of syntax, the quirks of grammar, the use of poetic license, and the richness of sound can never be fully captured in any translated rendition. My translation of these selected poems attempts only to render equivalencies in English in roughly the same idiomatic register that I perceive in Spanish. I have made no attempt in these poems to replicate Spanish meter and rhyme in English; to do so would do no credit to the poets nor offer any advantage to readers. In some cases, I add punctuation in English to facilitate the flow of meaning; in others, I respect the paucity of punctuation because it is clearly the poets' intent to do so. Footnotes are used sparingly, only for vocabulary and proper nouns that, even when faithfully translated, need further clarification. The *Introduction* to the work will hopefully provide a sufficient background for readers unfamiliar with Paraguay and to help situate the context of at least a significant number of the selected poetry.

ACKNOWLEDGEMENTS

This anthology could not have been brought to fruition without the generous support of a sabbatical leave and a faculty research grant from Ferris State University. I also wish to acknowledge the Council of International Exchange of Scholars for the senior Fulbright Award that permitted me to carry out the initial research for this project. Many thanks also to Gladys Carmagnola, Susy Delgado, and Ricardo de la Vega for their help in providing materials and historical background; to Gladys Gavilán of the library of the Casa de la Cultura; to Margarita Kallsen of the library of the Universidad Católica for providing me access to many otherwise inaccessible books; and to Professor Phillip Brewington Middleton for his close reading of the manuscript and his encouragement. Finally, my deepest thanks to poet Jacobo Rauskin, whose encyclopedic knowledge of world literature, of poetics, and of the Spanish and Guaraní languages and cultures were of immeasurable assistance. He graciously gave many hours of his time in reviewing translations, answering questions and offering encouragement in this project.

* * * * * * *

INTRODUCTION: CONTEXTUALIZING PARAGUAYAN POETRY

Familiarity with a poet's milieu—especially if it is a distant one—does not necessarily provide a reader with a special insight into the poet's poetics, intentions, or mystique. However, it does help to identify a context—in this case, Paraguayan—that is likely to be unknown to the majority of readers of this anthology. At the very least, this background will make it clear that these poets, in spite of the vast diversity of themes, styles, language, images, and perspectives, are products of very similar circumstances. In fact, within the relatively small cultural environment of Paraguay, most of the poets know (of) each other, and in many cases know each other's works. This introduction is for those readers who might not be familiar with this remote country.

GEOGRAPHY

Paraguay is about the size of California (157,048 square miles) and is landlocked by Bolivia, Brazil, and Argentina, close to the geographical center of South America. The Paraguay River, the principal waterway, cuts through the middle of the country from north to south and divides Paraguay into two distinct geographical regions. To the west is the Gran Chaco, an alluvial plain which is part of a vast area in central South

America, shared by Brazil, Paraguay, Bolivia, and Argentina. It is an inhospitable region, consisting of marshy plains, swamps, dry forests, and thorny scrubland; it is under-populated and underdeveloped, with few paved roads and cities. To the east of the Paraguay River is Paraguay proper, a more fertile region, consisting of low, wooded hills, rolling, grassy plains and a 1,000-2,000 ft. high plateau that extends north into Brazil. The plateau feeds numerous streams that flow westward through fertile hills and lowlands, eventually spilling into the Paraguay River. This area contains most of the country's population of over 6,000,000 and its economic livelihood. Asunción (548,000) is the capital and largest city, followed by Ciudad del Este (223,350), San Lorenzo (203,000), Luque (170,000), and Capiatá (154,000). Paraguay's climate is subtropical, with rainfall heavy in the Chaco summer, but evenly distributed in the rest of the country throughout the year.

ECONOMY

Outside of its fertile soil, its forests, and its wealth of rivers, Paraguay has few exploitable resources; even the tourism industry hasn't flourished. It has been one of South America's poorest countries, basing its economy largely on small-scale agriculture. Cassava, seed cotton, sugarcane, corn, wheat, sweet potatoes, *yerba mate* (a South American tea), bananas, and oranges are the leading crops. Livestock breeding (cattle, pigs, sheep, and horses) is also an important part of Paraguay's rural economy. Nearly half of Paraguay's labor force is employed in the agricultural sector, many of them farm on a subsistence basis. Although forest products have been a leading industry in Paraguay, injudicious management and illegal cutting have greatly depleted forests, causing ecological concern. Because of the scarcity of minerals, mining in Paraguay has never been significant. Manufacturing, limited to small companies concentrated in the Asunción area, produces packed meat, sugar, foodstuffs, and textiles.

Developmental problems in the economy have traditionally been attributed to official ineptitude and corruption, a shortage of skilled labor, inadequate transportation, all of which have traditionally accounted for a lack of international investment. An ambitious government program in the 1950s addressed these concerns by investing in improved roads, airports, river ports, and hydroelectric power. Although the country is landlocked, the Paraguay River accommodates ocean-going vessels, giving access to international trade. During the 1970s, the improvements in infrastructure stimulated a strong economy, but it was short lived, due to political instability, falling prices in commodities, foreign debt, and other problems during the 1980s and 1990s. The Itaipú hydroelectric dam—one of the world's largest—became operational in 1991, and has provided nearly all of Paraguay's electricity needs, enabling the export of power to neighboring countries. The joint Paraguayan-Argentine Yacyretá hydroelectric dam was completed in 1994, providing additional income for Paraguay.

In 2008, Paraguay's GDP was an estimated US$ 16 billion, and its GDP per capita (PPP) was an estimated $4,200, with services comprising 58.2 per cent of the total of the economy, industry 18.4 per cent, and agriculture and forestry combining for 23.4 per cent (2008 est.). As in the case of so many other developing countries, there is also an underground economy consisting of street vendors and small businesses dedicated to the resale of imported goods. Ciudad del Este has been known as the unofficial contraband capital of South America. Paraguay's total exports came to US$ 5.463 billion (2007 est.), and imports were US $9.172 billion (2008 est.). Paraguay is a founding member of MERCOSUR, a free trade association created in 1995 to foment trade and lower tariffs among fellow members Argentina, Uruguay, and Brazil.

HISTORY

The modern history of Paraguay begins around 1525, when Spanish and Portuguese expeditions seeking gold, explored the rivers in the area where they encountered peaceful tribes of the Guaraní. Conquest and colonization started soon after. In the 1600s, the Jesuits became very influential in the region, as they established numerous missions, called *reducciones*, in which they educated the Guaraní and other indigenous groups, converted them to Catholicism, and founded communities virtually independent of local and ecclesiastical rule. In 1750, Spain ceded Paraguayan territory—including seven *reducciones*—to Portugal, triggering an ill-fated Guaraní revolt, leading to the recall of the Jesuits from all of South America in 1767 and the dissipation of the missions. When Spain created the Viceroyalty of the Río de la Plata in 1776, with its seat in Buenos Aires, Paraguay was relegated to an insignificant border dependency.

Paraguay proclaimed its independence in 1811 and three years later José Gaspar Rodríguez de Francia declared himself dictator. He ruled absolutely until his death in 1840, but fearing an invasion from neighboring countries, the dictator instituted an isolationist policy for his new nation. When his nephew, Carlos Antonio López, became president and dictator in 1844, he reversed the isolationist policy, instituted governmental reorganization, and promoted commerce and the beginning of railroad construction. López was succeeded in the presidency by his son, Francisco Solano López, whose dream of a Paraguayan empire led Paraguay in 1865 into an ill-advised war against the alliance of Argentina, Brazil, and Uruguay. It resulted in a devastating defeat for Paraguay: the destruction of its national economy and agriculture; the loss of some 55,000 sq. mi. of territory; the occupation of the country by Brazilian forces until 1876; but most importantly, the loss of one-half of the Paraguayan population, including two-thirds of the adult males.

Following such catastrophic consequences of war, the nation spent the following decades in the reconstruction of commerce and agriculture, further complicated by instability in the government and social revolt. Between 1912 and 1923, there followed several presidential administrations that were able to promote peace and progress. In 1932, Paraguay and Bolivia went to war over a boundary dispute in the Chaco region; Paraguay was victorious, and the resulting 1938 peace treaty conceded to Paraguay about three-fourths of the disputed territory. A new constitution of 1940 provided for a reorganization of the government, including a centralization of federal power in the capital Asunción, which was intended to effect national economic and social reforms.

The next half century was dominated by dictators; but without the intervention of the military forces, the ouster of democratically elected presidents and the subsequent support of dictators would not have been possible. And so followed a succession of caudillos: General Higinio Morínigo (1940-1948); Federico Chávez, elected president in 1949, but who later imposed a dictatorship, and was re-elected to office in 1953, but overthrown by an army-police junta in 1954. However, it wasn't until General Alfredo Stroessner gained power, that the word "dictator" took on special significance. As commander-in-chief of the army and head of the Colorado Party he ran unopposed for the presidency in 1954, and not surprisingly won the election, and thereby began one of the longest-lasting dictatorships in modern history. Stroessner survived leftist takeover attempts and was reconfirmed president in 1958 by a plebiscite. His minions dominated the Congress, and together they effectively silenced all opposition to his iron-fisted rule by exiling or imprisoning leaders of opposing political parties and intellectuals, and banning news media critical of his government. So suffocating did life in Paraguay become, that thousands more went into voluntary exile. The General was re-elected in 1963, and after modifying the constitution to permit further re-elections, he was voted to continue his rule in 1968, and again in 1973, 1978, and 1983.

Under Stroessner's regime during the 1960s, some significant economic progress took place in Paraguay due to closer ties with neighboring countries, including a pact to develop the La Plata River Basin, the newly constructed Itaipú hydroelectric plant, and an effective check on rampant inflation. The mid-1980s experienced a period of civil liberalization, including the lifting of the state of siege in 1987, but as the economy worsened, a vocal opposition to the regime grew in strength and demanded further political freedoms and agrarian reform. Stroessner nevertheless was reelected to his eighth term in 1988, but he was ousted by a military revolt in 1989, led by General Andrés Rodríguez, who later that year was elected to the presidency. But neither Rodríguez, nor his successor Juan Carlos Wasmosy, (1993-1998) were able to turn around the weak economy, despite the privatization of state-owned enterprises, or Paraguay's joining the Southern Cone Common Market (MERCOSUR) in 1995.

In 1996, General Lino César Oviedo, commander of Paraguay's army, participated in a failed coup attempt against Wasmosy, but mysteriously got off unpunished. The populist general then decided to run for the presidency in 1997 and emerged as the Colorado party's candidate. However, shortly before the election, a military tribunal sentenced Oviedo to ten years in prison for his role in the coup attempt. Raúl Cubas Grau then became the Colorado party's candidate, won the election, and soon after pardoned Oviedo, an illegal act that prompted the Paraguayan Supreme Court to order Oviedo back to prison. Cubas ignored the Supreme Court order and allowed Oviedo to go free. Faced with impeachment, Cubas resigned as president and fled the country with Oviedo. In March 1999, Senate leader Luis González Machi was sworn in as president, but his term in office was marred by corruption.

In another colorful chapter of Paraguayan history, Nicanor Duarte Frutos of the Colorado party was elected in 2003 on a platform stressing economic recovery and a crackdown on corruption. He resigned on July 1, 2008 several months before the end of his term to become eligible to assume a position as senator in the Paraguayan legislature. His resignation resulted in a tumultuous legislative crisis, but Duarte eventually was named as a lifetime senator without salary and no voting power.

Fernando Armindo Lugo Méndez represents the latest in a long chain of unpredictable and controversial presidents. As a Roman Catholic bishop of the Diocese of San Pedro, he was known as "the bishop of the poor" because he supported peasant movements demanding a more favorable land distribution. Believing he could help the poor of the country more as an elected official, he resigned as ordinary in 2005, requested laicization of the Pope in order to run for office, but was denied permission. He nevertheless ran for the presidency under the banner of the Patriotic Alliance for Change, won the election in April 2008, and was sworn in as president, breaking a six-decade chain of the Colorado party's hold on the presidency. But his rise to power was not without controversy: legislators protested that the Paraguayan constitution forbids ministers of any religious denomination to hold elective office. Shortly after Lugo's swearing-in, the Catholic church finally acceded to his laicization. More controversy followed when three women came forth reporting that Lugo, during his service as bishop, had fathered three children. He admitted to fathering one of them and the other two cases were pending.

In spite of the predominance of iron-clad rule in so much of its history, Paraguay functions theoretically as a democracy. The nation is divided into seventeen departments and the capital district in Asunción. Each department has political autonomy, with a governor, a departmental council and a legislature. In national governance, the president, as the head-of-state and chief executive official, is limited to a single five-year term by a simple majority vote of the electorate. Paraguay's bicameral national legislature is composed of a forty-five-member senate and an eighty-member chamber of deputies. Legislators may serve terms of up to five years. The Asociación Nacional Republicana, (the Colorado Party), had been in power for sixty-one years before Lugo's victory. Other parties include the Christian Democratic Party, the Liberal Radical Party, the Authentic Liberal Radical Party, and the Liberal Party—all of which had traditionally offered token opposition—but the Alliance united a dozen parties to achieve victory. In spite of the stated reformist platforms of Paraguay's recent presidential candidates, the country has traditionally been besieged by official corruption, counterfeiting, contraband, money laundering, and organized crime.

SOCIETY

About 95% of Paraguayans are *mestizos* (of mixed Spanish and Native American ancestry), with small percentages of individuals of European descent, unassimilated *Guaraní*, and small colonies of immigrants from Japan, Korea, and Canada. German-speaking Mennonites form a notable immigrant group, settling mainly in the sparsely populated Chaco region in the west. Paraguay is a bilingual country: its official languages are Spanish and Guaraní, which is commonly spoken by about 90 per cent of the population. The overwhelming majority of Paraguayans live in the eastern third of the country. Approximately 43 per cent of its population live in rural areas, and the overall density of population is only about 16 persons per sq km (41 per sq mi), one of the lowest in South America.

A large majority of Paraguayans are Roman Catholic. Although elementary education is free and compulsory for children from ages six to fourteen, many children never complete their schooling for economic reasons. Upper secondary education and higher education are not free. The two major universities are the Catholic University (founded in 1960) and the National University of Asunción (1980). Although the literacy rate is estimated to be 94 per cent, there are a miniscule number of libraries in the country, and newspaper circulation is very limited. Paraguayans maintain strong ties with the Guaraní language, culture and the *Guaranía* (the typical music, featuring instruments used since pre-Colombian times). Along with Spanish, Guaraní is an official language of Paraguay. Indigenous motifs in arts and crafts are still popular throughout Paraguay. Of special note is the Ñandutí, a blend of Spanish lace and indigenous imagination. (See book cover.)

PARAGUAYAN WRITERS

In spite of severe limitations, Paraguayan narrative writers and poets—in self-exile or remaining in the country during the years of the Stroessner repression—continued writing what they had to write, sometimes suffering the consequences of imprisonment, torture, or even the euphemistic "missing" status. The poets selected for this anthology have all experienced the Stroessner years and have published works before, during and after the dictator's fall from power. Although some of the poems allude directly to life under the dictatorship, many others concern themselves with themes as traditional as poetry itself: the celebration of love, or the lamentation of its demise; the whole range of human emotions; nature; self-identity; everyday routine; familiar surroundings; evocation of the past or anticipation of the future; philosophical musings; and a self-reflected inquiry into the nature of poetry.

SOURCES

CIA World Factbook: <https://www.cia.gov/library/publications/the-world-factbook/geos/pa.html>

City Population of Paraguay: <http://www.citypopulation.de/Paraguay.html>

Encarta Encyclopedia: <http://encarta.msn.com/encyclopedia_761569154/Paraguay_(country).html>

Enciclopedia geográfica del Paraguay. La Nación (Asunción) Fascícula 3, no. 873.

Goodwin, Paul B. Jr. Global Studies: Latin America. 11th ed. Dubuque, Iowa:

McGraw- Hill/Dushkin, 2004; 12th ed. 2007.

<http://www.ethnologue.com/show_country.asp?name=Paraguay>

<http://www.factmonster.com/ipka/A0107879.html>

JOSÉ LUIS APPLEYARD

EL CEÑO DEL DICTADOR PERPETUO

¡Qué figura difícil!
¡Qué figura compleja!
Hay algo que me atrae en su ceño fruncido,
en su misión de Patria.

Fue honesto y minucioso,
honesto hasta en lo mínimo.
No fraguó su conquista con gestas libertarias,
pero hizo libre a un pueblo.
Duro, seco, inclemente hasta consigo mismo,
su única pasión fue un pueblo adolescente.

No fue ambiguo y su título de Dictador Perpetuo
lo recibió, valiente,
y con él gobernó como tal, con vigor de un asceta,
de un misógino puro
que impuso con su fría pasión de gobernante
el logro de su meta.

La historia aún no ha dictado
su fallo inapelable.
pero ya su figura se comienza a agrandar
en proporción directa al paso de los años.

Fue heridor de mi sangre, pero yo lo respeto:
cuando el Norte es tan alto,
no conviene aferrarse a privado recuerdo.

Seco, frío, implacable,
enigmático y triste,
su duro ceño indica no un carácter siniestro,
sino la voluntad hermética y tozuda
de liberar el suelo de tierra prometida
que es simplemente el nuestro.

El labio y la palabra

SOLAMENTE LOS AÑOS

Solamente los años nos permiten
conocer lo que acaso fue secreto,
los años nos invaden y nos dicen,

THE SCOWL OF THE PERPETUAL DICTATOR

What a difficult countenance!
What a complex countenance!
There's something that draws me to his furrowed brow,
on his patriotic mission.

He was honest and meticulous,
honest in the smallest detail.
He didn't forge his conquest with anarchistic exploits,
but he freed a nation.
Hard, dry, severe even with himself,
his only passion was an adolescent country.

He wasn't ambiguous; his title of Perpetual Dictator
he welcomed, valiantly,
with it he ruled as such, with ascetic vigor,
as a pure misogynist
who imposed with his pure passion of rule
the realization of his goal.

History has not yet declared
its final verdict
but his stature is beginning to grow
in direct proportion to the passing of the years.

He wounded my blood, but I respect him:
when the goal is so lofty
it's not worth insisting on private memories.

Dry, cold, implacable,
enigmatic and sad,
his hard brow reveals no evil character,
rather the impenetrable and stubborn will
to liberate the ground of the promised land
that is simply ours.

El labio y la palabra

ONLY THE YEARS

Only the years permit us
to know what was perhaps a secret,
the years invade us, they inform us,

qué poco resta, qué transido hueco
aparece después de las murallas.
Lo que queda otra vez es campo abierto,
una carne, una sonrisa declinante,
alguna trayectoria, la tristeza
de comprobar –no ya Tomás—las llagas
de un rostro que no fue, de una vileza
que engalanadas formas de un domingo
la hicieron como es, sólo una mueca.

Solamente los años

LAS PALABRAS

A veces hay palabras que se mueren
y no las resucita el diccionario;
palabras simples, claras, que acrecieron
el verbo de la infancia en nuestros labios.
En balde las buscamos para darles
una vida que ha muerto con los años.

Dulces palabras nuestras exiliadas,
sólo sonido ya desamparado,
que por un tiempo fueron los mojones
de nuestro personal vocabulario.
Es inútil buscarlas, ya se han muerto
bajo el peso brutal del diccionario.

Entonces era siempre

LAPACHO*

Copa de vino añejo que desborda
la sutil embriaguez de sus colores,
encaje, cromo y luz en el que bordan
los pájaros la gloria de sus flores.

Mano morena que enguantada en lila
acaricia el azul de las mañanas,
badajo florecido de la esquila
triunfal del firmamento que se inflama.

Mancha de luz al borde de un camino,
jalón del campo y corazón del viento,
árbol que tiene para sí el destino
de ser la primavera en todo tiempo.

how little remains, what a wretched emptiness
appears after the walls have fallen.
Again, what remains is wide open:
flesh, a declining smile,
some unknown path, the sadness
of confirming—no doubting Thomas—the ulcers
of an inexistent face, of a villainy
forged by the decorated protocol
of a Sunday, just a grimace.

Solamente los años

THE WORDS

At times there are words that die,
the dictionary doesn't resuscitate them;
simple words, clear, that increased
the infant's lexicon on our lips.
In vain do we search for them to give them
a life that has died with the years.

Our exiled words are so sweet,
only sounds, now helpless,
that for a while were landmarks
of our personal vocabulary.
It's useless to look for them, they have died
under the brutal weight of the dictionary.

Entonces era siempre

LAPACHO*

A glass of aged wine that overflows
the subtle intoxication of its colors,
lace, chrome and light where the birds
embroider the glory of its flowers.

Dark hand gloved in lilac
caresses the blue of the mornings,
flowery clapper of heaven's triumphal
bell bursting into flames.

Spot of light alongside a road,
range pole, heart of the wind,
tree that takes onto itself the destiny
of being spring at all times.

Y ya solo en la tarde pura y bella,
embriagado de luces y colores,
es el árbol que enciende las estrellas
con la llama morada de sus flores.

*Árbol bignoniáceo común en Paraguay y en otros países de latitud similar.

Tomado de la mano

COLOFÓN

Todo puede volver,
pero este amargo corazón de patios,
esta víscera ardiente que revuelca
su agónica vivencia entre la sangre,
que late, sueña, duele y se desvela,
este pedazo viejo de mi carne
adherida a un pasado,
apretujada a él como en un beso,
hacinante de ayeres,
adustamente mía,
esta víscera trágica y absurda
que se está yendo siempre
y que se aferra,
este pedazo de mi vida en siempre
necesita y no puede
regresar.

Huyen las tardes,
laten los veranos,
los perros muerden el osario cárdeno
de la desesperación de los crepúsculos.
Las viejas cuentas de gastados brillos
amparan la mudez de los rosarios,
la tarde, el tiempo, el sol, la lluvia, el viento,
las palabras amargas,
los ojos que miraban y se han ido
y dentro de mí mismo,
crepitante,
este reloj de carne que se muere,
que sigue yendo siempre,
que sigue trajinando,
este pedazo de mi vida en siempre
necesita y no puede regresar.

Entonces era siempre

And now alone in the afternoon, pure and fair,
intoxicated with lights and colors,
it's the tree that lights the stars
with the purple flame of its flowers.

*A bignonieaceous tree common in Paraguay and countries of similar latitude.

Tomado de la mano

COLOPHON

Everything can return,
but this bitter heart of patios,
these burning viscera that trample
their agonizing experience in the blood
that beat, dream, hurt and keep vigil,
this old piece of my flesh
stuck to a past,
pressed together with it as in a kiss,
a stacking up of yesterdays,
grimly mine,
these tragic and absurd viscera
that are always taking leave
and yet cling on,
this piece of my life in a place called Always
needs to return,
but is unable.

The afternoons flee,
the summers pulsate,
the dogs bite the purplish ossuary
of the desperation of dusk.
The old beads, no longer shiny,
protect the muteness of the rosaries,
the afternoon, the time, the sun, the rain, the wind,
the bitter words,
the eyes that have seen and have gone,
and within myself,
crepitating,
this clock of dying flesh,
that always goes on and on,
that goes rushing about,
this piece of my life in a place called Always
needs to return, but is unable.

Entonces era siempre

HAY UN SITIO

Hay un sitio en el mundo donde vivo
pequeño y singular,
un sitio mío,
un pedazo de tierra con olor a madera,
con gentes como yo,
en diminuto, sangrante y triste
corazón cautivo.

Un pedazo de tierra, pocos hombres,
y un alfange de acero como río.
Yo estoy en él, soy parte de esa parte
minúscula del mundo. Tengo amigos
que comparten el tiempo y lo desangran
con lentitud, sin prisa, desde antiguo.

La vida es muy sencilla,
sólo basta
ser fiel el cumplimiento de los ritos:
matar a la verdad cada mañana
y dejarla morir cada domingo.
Quien conoce la clave, dulcemente
puede vivir tranquilo en este sitio.
Las palabras mantienen la tersura
de su forma redonda y sin resquicios,
pero aquello que encierran por ser verbo
en cada labio da un sabor distinto.

La gramática es tensa, diferente
de toda similar. Sólo el sonido
de sus vocablos tiene semejanza
con un idioma al que llamara mío.

Hay sinónimos claros, transparentes:
ser libre es vegetar sin albedrío,
robar es trabajar, amor es odio,
y vivir es morir desguarnecido.
La soledad se llama compañía
y el traicionar, ser fiel a los amigos.
La novedad, vejez. Todo lo nuevo
tiene una oscura pátina de antiguo.

Hay un sitio en el mundo donde vivo
pequeño y singular.
Un sitio mío,

THERE'S A PLACE

There's a place in the world where I live
small and unique,
a place of my own,
a piece of land, redolent of wood,
with people like me,
in a captive heart,
diminutive, bleeding and sad.

A piece of earth, few men,
and a steel scimitar like a river.
I am in it, I'm part of that
miniscule part of the world. I have friends
who share time and bleed it dry,
slowly, unhurried, since long ago.

Life is very simple
all that's needed
is faithful compliance with the rites:
killing the truth every morning
and leaving it die every Sunday.
He who knows the key, can live
in this place sweetly and tranquilly.
Words maintain the fluidity
of their form, round and without cracks,
but all that they enclose as language
on every lip gives a distinct flavor.

The grammar is tense, different
from any other. Only the sound
of the words has a semblance
to a language which I might call mine.

There are clear, transparent synonyms:
to be free is to vegetate indifferently,
to steal is to work, love is hatred,
and to live is to die all dismantled.
Loneliness is called company
and to betray is to be faithful to one's friends.
Novelty, old age. Everything new
has an obscure patina of antique.

There's a place in the world where I live
small and unique.
A place of my own,

un pedazo de tierra que se pudre,
con gente como yo,
de diminuto, sangrante y triste
corazón cautivo.

El sauce permanece y tres motivos

JUGLAR DE LO PEQUEÑO

Yo siempre he sido juglar de lo pequeño.
He cantado a los grillos y a su canto,
a las hormigas ágiles, al viento
y a ese dolor que lucha y es el tiempo.
Nunca podré internarme en paralelos
de abstracciones solemnes y baratas
que encubren la ignorancia y la devuelven
envuelta en celofanes de jactancia.
Prefiero los minutos que dejaron
su impronta en el recuerdo y deshicieron
los falsos preconceptos del olvido
proyectándose al tiempo de lo sido.
Círculo eterno, noria permanente
sobre un eje de vida dando vueltas
una vez y otra vez en el momento
huyente y regresante y conocido,
cambiante siempre y siempre repetido,
en recuerdo profético del todo,
agua que forma la unidad del río,
siendo la misma y siempre diferente
hormiga de mi canto, cigarra decisiva;
en ayeres-mañanas del presente
voy a tumbos muriendo y esta vida
de cansancio y estímulo se vuelve
alfa enlazada en comunión constante
con esa omega pura de la muerte.

Juglar de lo pequeño

a piece of land that rots,
with people like me,
in a captive heart,
diminutive, bleeding and sad.

El sauce permanece y tres motivos

MINSTREL OF THE LITTLE THINGS

I have always been a minstrel of little things.
I have sung to the crickets and to their song,
to the agile ants, to the wind
and to that suffering that struggles and is time itself.
I'll never be able to get into comparisons
of solemn and cheap abstractions
that cover up ignorance and return it
covered in the cellophane of arrogance.
I prefer the minutes that left
their impression on my memory and undid
the false preconceptions of oblivion
projecting themselves on the time of what has been.
Eternal circle, permanent treadmill
upon an axis of life going round and round
again and again in every moment
fleeing, returning and always known,
changing always and always repeated,
in a prophetic memory of everything,
water that forms the unity of the river,
being the same and always different,
the ant of my song, the decisive cicada;
in the yesterdays-tomorrows of the present
I'm tumbling to death and this life
of fatigue and stimulus becomes
the alpha tied in constant communion
with the pure omega of death.

Juglar de lo pequeño

II

Atardecido ya, como este día
me enfrento a la falange de recuerdos.
Unos, ya muy lejanos, se interponen
y develan sus cándidos secretos.
Secretos que lo fueron bajo un techo
que los cubrió con cómplices derechos.
Sombras de algún desván, humo sin fuego,
pesadillas pasadas de algún sueño,
y así como han venido, ya se han ido
como deben hacerlo los desechos.
Vienen otros recuerdos, más cercanos,
que ofrecen realidades como ejemplos.

Cenizas de la vida

II

Approaching late afternoon, just like today,
I confront a phalanx of memories.
Some, now very distant, intervene
and reveal their candid secrets.
They were secrets then, under a roof,
that covered them with upright accomplices.
Shadows of some attic, smoke without fire,
and just as they have come, so they have gone
just as debris must behave.
Other memories come, more intimate,
that offer realities as examples.

Ashes of Life

MONCHO AZUAGA

ARTE POÉTICA

Que ya no escriba.
Que ya no hable, me pidieron.
Que calle.
Que todo es inútil, me dijeron.
Que no vale la pena tanto esfuerzo.
Sin embargo,
afuera, en la calle,
voces anónimas, sombras, casi sombras
reclamaban el viento, la lluvia azul,
el cielo.

Bajo los vientos del sur

RESIGNACIÓN

Aunque sea únicamente el silencio,
aunque el silencio únicamente quede,
deja crecer a las golondrinas y los girasoles,
deja a la rana engañarse de luna con el camalote,
qué importa que sea el silencio el que se tiña de agrio,
qué importa sentir la lengua rota de quebrar
silencios inquebrantables.
Deja entonces al silencio.
Porque, ¿quiénes son los que se sienten al borde del incendio?
¿Quiénes son los que hombrean hambre secuestrando mariposas?
¿Acaso nos miramos las manos
cuando están mojadas de silencio?
En verdad, arrugamos los años
para que se acabe el tiempo.
Deja entonces al silencio.
Deja morir al sonido en los umbrales vacíos de la luz.
Deja en la sencillez el vuelo quieto de las hojas amarillas,
Qué importa que sea Octubre el mes de las celdas,
qué importa aquí o allá si el amor y la muerte
se hacen de la misma manera.
Deja entonces al silencio.
Aunque solamente sea él.
Aunque únicamente él habite entre Nosotros.

Bajo los vientos del sur

POETICS

Don't write any more.
Don't speak any more, they asked me.
Shut up.
Everything's useless, they told me.
All that effort isn't worth it.
Nevertheless,
outside, in the street,
anonymous voices, shadows, almost shadows
demanded the wind, the blue rain,
the sky.

Bajo los vientos del sur

RESIGNATION

Even if it's only silence,
even if only silence remains,
let the swallows and the sunflowers grow,
let the frog confuse the moon with a water hyacinth.
Who cares if it is silence that embitters itself,
who cares if your tongue feels broken from breaking
unbreakable silences?
So leave silence alone.
Because, who are they that feel the fire's singe?
Who are they that bear hunger by kidnapping butterflies?
Do we really look at our hands
when they're soaked in silence?
We truly wrinkle the years
to do away with time.
So leave silence alone.
Let sounds die in the empty thresholds of light.
Leave the quiet flight of the yellow leaves in its innocence.
What does it matter if October is the month for jails?
What does it matter, here or there, if love and death
are carried out in the same manner?
Let silence be.
Even if it is just silence.
Even if it alone dwells among us.

Bajo los vientos del sur

CIUDAD SITIADA

Detenida la ciudad,
endurecidos los zaguanes,
las alcobas y las calles
es de piedra el aire.

Mera roca,
basalto, granito,
molestia de carne y miedo,
la vida.

Y el amor, paloma imposible
aplastada contra el cielo.

Muda sombra la noche
Lágrima seca el alma.
Descompuesta la palabra,
hedionda la lengua,
secuestraron el alba.

Alambradas y muros,
hierros, órdenes, decretos.
Silencio, duro silencio.
La ciudad en calma.
La Paz.

...y al sol tendidas las iguanas.

Ciudad sitiada

CIPRIANO BENITEZ, Doctor

No leyó nunca las aventuras de Jesse James.
No sabía de libros ni de revistas
ni vio películas de violencia.
No cantó canciones de guerra.
Nunca su mano acarició el rostro del fusil,
no tuvo edad.
Sólo conoció la dura tierra,
la cosecha esquiva
y el sol de enero sobre su pecho desnudo.
Creyó en el Dios Justo,
en la bendición de la lluvia sobre los surcos.
Vivió descalzo. Se persignó ante el pombero.

CITY UNDER SIEGE

The city is under arrest,
hardened are the doorways,
the alcoves and the streets,
the air is made of stone.

Just rock,
basalt, granite,
a nuisance of flesh and fear,
life.

And love, an impossible dove
crushed against the sky.

The night, a silent shadow
The soul, a dry tear.
The word is out of order,
language is insufferable,
they kidnapped the dawn.

Barbed wire and walls,
shackles, orders, decrees.
Silence, hard silence.
All quiet in the city.
Peace.

...and the iguanas stretched out in the sun.

Ciudad sitiada

CIPRIANO BENITEZ, Doctor

He never read the adventures of Jesse James
He knew nothing of books nor magazines
nor did he see violent movies.
He didn't sing songs of war.
His hand never caressed the face of a gun,
he was ageless.
He only knew the hard earth,
the evasive crop
and January's sun on his bare chest.
He believed in a Just God,
in the blessing that rain brought to his furrows.
He walked barefoot. Made the sign of the cross
when meeting the forest elf.

Fueron sus días, trabajo y horizonte.
Fueron sus noches, descanso y estrellas.
Largas sequías no mataron su esperanza.
Murió antes, de treinta balas,
mirando el lucero, una madrugada.
Después,
los diarios dijeron que predicaba el odio,
que no respetó nunca el progreso ni la paz,
que distribuía panfletos subversivos
y que lecturas foráneas le extraviaron el corazón.
Libros prohibidos de su extensa biblioteca,
cartas de líderes lejanos,
poemas de su pulso y pluma
y armas y canciones de sangre para la Patria
mostró el noticiero de la Televisión.
Cipriano Benítez, 16 años, agricultor,
no supo nunca
que después de su muerte
le llamarían Doctor,
caudillo de una sofocada revolución.

Ciudad sitiada

DESAPARECIDO

De hurras, vivas y consignas.
De metrallas, piedras y torturas.
De tanques, bombas y cuchillos
hicieron la patria.
La llenaron de sombras y miedo,
de soplones y retratos.
Escribieron la Historia
y borraron de ella el alba.

Del aire hicieron monedas de odio
y lunas de sangre anochecieron nuestras ventanas
Descompusieron las palabras.
Asaltaron mi casa,
leyeron mis cartas,
interpretaron mis sueños
y los cuentos de mi infancia.

El partido puso adjetivos a mi nombre
y un número fijo en mis espaldas.
Y a duro fierro desangraron la mañana.

His days were work and horizon.
His nights were repose and stars.
Long droughts didn't dash his hopes.
He died before that, from thirty bullets,
gazing at the morning star, early one morning.
Afterwards,
the newspapers said he preached hatred,
he never respected progress nor peace,
he distributed subversive leaflets
and outside influences misled his heart.
Banned books from his extensive library,
letters from distant leaders,
poems from his own pen
and arms and songs of blood shed for one's Country
all of this on TV's nightly news.
Cipriano Benítez, sixteen years old, farmer,
never found out
that after his death
they would call him Doctor,
leader of a failed revolution.

Ciudad sitiada

MISSING

From hoorays, cheers and slogans.
From machine guns, stones and torture.
From tanks, bombs and knives
they forged the fatherland.
They filled it with shadows and fear,
with informers and portraits.
they wrote 'The' History
and from it they erased the dawn.

From thin air they made the coins of hatred
and bloody moons greeted the night through our windows
They decomposed words.
They broke into my house,
They read my letters,
interpreted my dreams
and the stories of my infancy.

The party applied adjectives to my name
and a prison number on my back
and with hard irons they bled the morning to death.

Hablaron en Congresos Internacionales,
sonrieron en las fotografías,
en diarios y noticieros
juraron y se persignaron,
vistiéronse de blanco
y definitivamente todo, todo lo olvidaron.

Nadie recordó a mi mujer llorando
Nadie respondió a las preguntas de mis hijos
Nadie supo de mis libros.
Tan sólo la gaceta oficial
en amplia lista dijo: elemento antisocial.

Y sellaron: Desaparecido

Ciudad sitiada

GENERACIÓN DE LA PAZ

Aprendimos a callar
a bajar la cabeza y sonreír,
a no mirar y callar
y repetir:
        qué hermoso es vivir
        qué hermoso es vivir
        qué hermoso es vivir!

Luces de colores,
pantallas de neón,
miriñaques en las vidrieras,
palomas de cartón.

Jueces siempre en venta
togas de perfecto inglés,
contrabando, tortura y drogas
Primavera al revés!

Aprendimos a callar
a evitar líos y no gritar
y ciegos nos morimos
hartos de tanta Paz!

Aprendimos a callar
a vendernos y adular
caprichos del mandamás.

They spoke at international conferences,
they smiled in photographs,
in newspapers and in news programs
they swore oaths and made the sign of the cross,
they dressed in white
and they forgot everything, just everything.

Nobody remembered my wife crying.
Nobody answered my children's questions.
Nobody discovered my books.
The official gazette
in a long account said only: an antisocial type.

And they stamped: Missing.

Ciudad sitiada

THE GENERATION OF PEACE

We learned how to shut up,
to lower our heads and to smile,
not to look up and to be quiet
and repeat:
    how beautiful it is to live
    how beautiful it is to live
    how beautiful it is to live!

Colored lights,
neon signs,
trinkets in the show windows,
cardboard doves.

Judges always for sale
togas of perfect English cloth
contraband, torture and drugs
Spring in reverse!

We learned to shut up
to avoid trouble and not to shout
and we died blindly
sick and tired of so much Peace!

We learned to be quiet
to sell ourselves and to flatter
the caprices of the big boss.

Aprendimos a callar
futuro de la patria
Generación de la Paz.

—Silencio! ¿Quién habla?
—Nadie vive. Son hurras
por su orden, ¡mi General!

Paraíso silencioso
hermosa Tierra Sin Mal
mudos, ciegos y sordos
hasta el Juicio Final!

Ciudad Sitiada

ADAN

Ya no quiero el viejo paraíso amazónico
ni aspiro a las manzanas ni a los abedules
ni al cielo claro de las estampas
ni a las nubes ni a los ríos largos y azules
ni a las bucólicas pretensiones de animales
posando ante la vergonzosa Eva

en vano me tientas con ese aburrido paraíso

yo asciendo a los cielos
o bajo despacio en ascensores transparentes
en silenciosas escaleras mecánicas
y admiro la piel de las serpientes
en los cintos que cuelgan en las vidrieras

y ángel o demonio,
mato o muero en los divertidos video games
ay, mentiras bíblicas,
huertos sexuales

Adán en el shopping no está solo
juego con hermosos muchachos
y niñas de alquiler
y bailo
y mancho mis labios con rojos pimientos
la tarde es divina con hamburguesas y rock
y esa charla entrecortada de muchachas
preparando el próximo minuto de amor

We learned to shut up,
we, the future of the country,
the Generation of Peace.

"Silence! Who's speaking?"
"No one. They're just cheers
as you ordered, my General!"

Silent paradise
beautiful Flawless Land
deaf, dumb and blind
till Judgment Day!

Ciudad sitiada

ADAM

I no longer want the old Amazon paradise
nor do I aspire to the apples nor the birches
nor the clear sky of illustrations
nor the clouds, nor the long, blue rivers
nor the bucolic desires of animals
posing before the shameful Eve

in vain you tempt me with that boring paradise

I ascend to the heavens
or descend slowly on transparent escalators
on silent mechanical steps
and admire the skin of the serpents
on the belts hanging in showcases

and angel or demon
I kill or I die in the amusing video games
oh, Biblical lies
sexual orchards

Adam in the mall isn't alone
I play with handsome boys
and girls for hire
and I dance
and color my lips with red peppers
the afternoon is divine with hamburgers and rock
and that intermittent chatter of girls
preparing for the next minute of love

quien tienta a mi corazón
con espléndidas propagandas?

Dios está en el televisor
anunciando ventas, guerras
y un modernísimo aerosol.

Shopping, Shopping,
toda la sed de mi alma.
Coca Cola la calma,
y un poco de coquéin.

Naidopori problema, Adán
beautiful brothers, wee queen!!!

inédito, 1999

GUERRA

La muerte llega desde el mar,
Desde el cielo más oscuro
Solloza un niño
En los vientos del Afganistán

Cabalga el dolor
En el Center World
Y un negro aúlla
Y estalla el sol

Satélites violentos
Amputan mi canción
Misiles ciegos
Matan a mi Dios

Cómo explicar la razón de la poesía
En medio de tanto dolor
Sorprendido estoy cantando
En el corazón de la muerte,
En el reino del horror

(La guerra en casa
En un dulce programa de televisión)
Ay, mis muertos de Nueva Yorki
Llora el niño de Afganistán
Y enmudece mi canción.

inédito, 2002

who tempts my heart
with splendid propaganda?

God is on TV
announcing sales, wars
and the latest aerosol.

Shopping, Shopping,
all my soul's thirst.
Coca Cola calms it,
and a bit of cocaine.

There's no problem, Adam,
beautiful brothers, whoa, queen!!!

Unpublished, 1999

WAR

Death arrives from the sea,
From the darkest sky
A child sobs
In the winds of Afghanistan

Grief mounts
in the World Trade Center
And a black man howls
And blows up the sun

Violent satellites
Amputate my song
Blind missiles
Kill my God

How does one explain the reason for poetry
In the midst of so much suffering
I am surprised, singing
In the heart of death,
In the reign of horror

(The war at home
On a sweet television program)

Oh, all my dead in New York
A child cries in Afghanistan
And my song turns mute.

Unpublished, 2002

GLADYS CARMAGNOLA

TRUEQUE

Peces hinchados y deformes
—los recuerdos—
penetran en el hueco de una herida
y se quedan
y viven su existencia trágica, incorpórea,
castigando con su peso invisible
el hogar que han tomado por asalto.

Cuando la herida cicatrice,
uno,
al menos uno seguirá viviendo
deforme y gigantesco
hinchado pez que todo lo devora
con sus agudos dientes y su cólera.

Oye:
yo no puedo contigo.
Apártate de mí
o por lo menos dime tu nombre.

Dime
al menos la primera letra de este dolor
y toma luego
en mí otra vez—¡qué importa!—
el precio que requieras por tu nombre.

Un verdadero hogar

CONSECUENCIA

Alguna madrugada
salí sola a la calle
a pasear, simplemente.

¡No me mires así!

Tú sabes que hace falta
aire puro,
libertad total,
después de tanto involuntario, empecinado encierro,
No. No ha quedado allí
la aventura inocente:

EXCHANGE

Bloated and deformed fish
—memories—
penetrate in the gap of a wound
and remain
and live their tragic existence, incorporeal,
punishing with their invisible weight
the home that they have overtaken.

When the wound heals,
one,
at least one, will continue living,
deformed and gigantic,
a bloated fish that devours everything
with its sharp teeth, its fury.

Listen:
I can't put up with you.
Get away from me,
or at least give me your name.

Tell me
at least the first letter of that suffering
and then take
from me again—who cares?—
the price that you require for your name.

Un verdadero hogar

CONSEQUENCE

One morning, in the wee small hours,
I went out on the street
to take a walk, that's all.

Don't look at me that way!

You know we need
fresh air,
total freedom,
after such an involuntary, persistent confinement.
No. The innocent adventure
hasn't stopped there:

los perros del vecino
oliscaron mis pasos
y ladran desde entonces,
indefinidamente.

Un verdadero hogar

CUENTO

Había una vez
un león, valeroso, inteligente
se pasaba la vida
caminando amistoso entre la gente;
no alardeaba nunca
ni de ser generoso ni valiente.

El podía ser así
porque realmente
era de virtuoso corazón
y de cerebro vivo y brazos fuertes.

Había una vez
(dos, 100.000 veces)
un león que no existió
y me parece
que nunca existirá
porque los fuertes
que yo conozco aquí
son imprudentes
y se pasan la vida
—casi siempre—
alardeando de virtudes
inexistentes
y podríamos arriesgarnos a llamarlos animales
simplemente.

Comencemos así:

Había una vez
(ya no sé cuántas veces)
voraces animales y dañinos insectos
mezclados, confundidos, inevitablemente
—si no, será desgracia—
entre la gente.

the neighbor's dogs
sniffed at my steps
and have been barking ever since,
indefinitely.

Un verdadero hogar

A STORY

Once upon a time,
a courageous, intelligent lion
spent his life
walking amicably among the people;
he never boasted about
being generous or valiant.

He could be that way
because he really had
a virtuous heart,
a lively brain and strong legs.

Once upon a time,
(twice, a 100,000 times)
there was a lion that didn't exist
and, I believe,
that never will exist
because the strong ones
I know here
are imprudent
and spend their life
—almost always—
bragging about their non-existent
virtues
and we could dare calling them animals,
quite simply.

Let's begin this way:

Once upon a time
(I don't know how many times)
voracious animals and harmful insects
were mixed in and inevitably blended
—if not, how unfortunate—
with people.

¿Que cómo yo lo sé?
Porque el cuento sucede justo enfrente.

Y aunque tú no lo ves,
sé que lo entiendes.

Igual que en las capueras

CUESTIÓN DE AMOR

En este afán de arar y sembrar sílabas
ya no indago por qué ni para qué.
Cuestión de amor, digámosle.
O de necesidad, podría ser.

Igual que en las capueras,
en este irremediable menester
—sea magra o abundante nuestra siembra—
dejamos, cuando menos, parte de nuestra piel.

Igual que en las capueras, la cosecha
no siempre sacia el hambre ni la sed.

Dios te bendiga, hermano, por creerme:
Eres hombre de fe.

Igual que en las capueras

DONDE ESCONDERME

Nunca podré afirmar
que me interese un ápice tu suerte

Con decirte que hoy fui a visitar
el común domicilio de la muerte
buscando algún lugar de 1 X 2
donde esconderme
cuando ya todo sea para mí
indiferente.

Me importa en realidad, cuanto sucede,
demasiado, innecesariamente.

Banderas y señales

How do I know this?
Because the story takes place right in front of us.

And even if you don't see it,
I know you will understand.

Igual que en las capueras

A MATTER OF LOVE

In this chore of plowing and seeding syllables
I no longer inquire about the whys and wherefores.
It's a matter of love, let's say.
Or of necessity, it could be that.

Like on farmland,
in this irremediable job
—whether the sowing is meager or abundant—
we leave, at the very least, part of our flesh.

Like on farmland, the harvest
doesn't always sate hunger or thirst.

God bless you, brother, for believing me:
You are a man of faith.

Como en las capueras

SOMEWHERE TO HIDE

I'll never be able to say
that your fate interests me one iota.

Let me tell you that today I went to visit
death's shared domicile
searching for a place 1 x 2 meters
where I can hide
when everything becomes
indifferent to me.

In reality, everything that happens matters to me,
too much, unnecessarily.

Banderas y señales

¡MENTIRA!

No. No es verdad que siempre
el tiempo todo lo mitigue.
Yo no debí saber de fusilados.
No debí oír de "fuerzas revolucionarias..."
No.
No debió haber habido...
No debí comprender qué es pynandi,
que se saquea, se viola, se incendia, se degüella...
No debí cobijar en la memoria
el olor de la sangre en el hermoso rostro mate de mi abuela
ni ver la bayoneta calada en el pecho desnudo de mi madre.
No.
No debí escuchar el reiterado
silbido de las balas.
No debí contemplar el fuego aquella noche
trepar de nuestro hogar directo al cielo.
No debí arropar entre mis brazos
un bebé de capucha celeste humedecida por las lágrimas
mientras mi madre alzaba a mi otra hermana
y un hervidor de leche tibia
iba dejando rastros al enemigo.
Como en Hansel y Gretel, Mamá.

Por suerte está mi hermano.
—¿Y Papá?
—Ya vendrá.
Después sabría que a él lo habían arrojado
"por las dudas nomás", a un calabozo.

¿Quién es "el enemigo", Mamá?
Y ... quizá nuestro hermano.
Ese vecino
que mancilló la mesa uno que otro domingo.

Así empezó para mi corazón
el verdadero exilio.

Nadie merece estos recuerdos que hoy te pido
me ayudes a arrojar
a la otra orilla.

Territorio esmeralda

¡LIE!

No. It's not true that everything
is healed with time..
I shouldn't have known about shootings.
I shouldn't have heard the "revolutionary forces."
No.
There shouldn't have been any...
I shouldn't have understood what "shoeless" means,
nor about plunder, rape, burnings, throat-cutting...
I shouldn't have harbored in my memory
the smell of blood on my grandmother's beautiful face
nor seen the bayonet piercing my mother's bare breast.
No.
I shouldn't have heard the repeated
whistle of the bullets.
I shouldn't have witnessed the fire that night
climbing from our home straight to heaven.
I shouldn't have had to wrap in my arms
a sky-blue hooded baby soaked in tears
while my mother carried my other sister
and a pot of warm milk
that was leaving a trail for the enemy.
Like in Hansel and Gretel, Mother.

Luckily, my brother's here.
"And father?"
"He'll be along."
Later, I'd find out they had thrown him
into a dungeon "just in case."

Who is "the enemy," Mother?
Well. . . maybe our brother.
That neighbor
who stained the table one Sunday back.

That's how the real exile
began for my heart.

No one deserves these memories
the ones that today I beg you
to help me hurl to the other shore.

Territorio esmeralda

MÁS QUE RÍO

Saber que remontamos, más que un río,
un océano henchido de borrascas,
capeando olas donde zozobraron
tenaces moradores de una balsa
que sigue, porque allá, en el horizonte
se divisa el perfil de una comarca
donde quizá unas manos se nos tiendan
a dar o recibir una migaja
y tal vez haya un techo que nos libre
de la intemperie, donde en una cama
reposen piel y huesos, y la sangre
se entibie al abrazo de las mantas
y podamos vivir esa oración
que más que modulando letras vanas
se reza con las sílabas nacidas
en el único bote hacia el mañana.

Saber que navegamos ese océano. . .
que simplemente no hay una ensenada;
que el abismo es profundo,
y las islas, escasas;
que la aldea, si existe, está ¡tan lejos!
que la sal nos perfora las entrañas
y hay sólo una oración
'un mendrugo nomás' . . . 'un poco de agua". . .

Río blanco y antiguo

MORE THAN A RIVER

Know that we went upstream, more than just a river,
an ocean swollen by storms,
weathering waves where tenacious
sojourners foundered in a raft
that still moves on, because there, in the horizon
we can make out the profile of a province
where some hands might reach out to us
to give or receive some crumbs,
and perhaps there's a roof to shelter us
from the foul weather, where we can
rest our skin and bones, and where our blood
can warm under the embrace of blankets,
and we are able to live out this prayer
which, more than just modulating vain letters,
we can pray with syllables born
in the only boat bound for tomorrow.

Know that we sail that ocean. . .
that there is simply no harbor;
that the abysm is deep,
the islands scarce
and the town, if it exists, is so far away,
that the salt perforates our innards
and there is only this prayer
'just a crust of bread' . . . 'a little water' . . .

Río blanco y antiguo

SUSY DELGADO

7

Yo
estoy aquí y espero.
Trasunto soledad y aburrimiento.
Conceptualizo y crezco
de acuerdo a mi tiroides.
Uso una libertad
empaquetada y esterilizada.

Estoy cansada de decir "tal vez"
de reincidir en el cansancio
y tal vez, de esperar . . .

Algún extraviado temblor

22

Estoy a punto
de escribir un poema
donde voy a decirte
que si llegada al próximo arrebato
tus manos grandes y calientes
no me rescatan de este frío,
puedo morirme sin remedio.

Algún extraviado temblor

28

Y sin embargo estoy aquí.
Resbalada en este escenario de sordos relojes.
Perfectamente distraída.
Con un vago recuerdo de caballos liberados al viento.
Con el presentimiento vago de una muerte acechando en las esquinas.
No tengo ganas de fingirme
asentada en mi propia baldosa.
Estoy improvisando todavía
lo que apenas intuyo.
Además,
tengo una capacidad desmesurada
de olvidar, sospechar, desorientarme,
repartirme, perderme y desorganizarlo todo.
Por eso a veces, me despierto desnuda,

7

I
am here and I wait.
I copy loneliness and boredom.
I conceptualize and grow
according to my thyroid.
I use a liberty
all packaged and sterilized.

I'm tired of saying 'perhaps,'
of falling back into fatigue
and perhaps, of waiting . . .

Algún extraviado temblor

22

I'm just about
to write a poem
in which I'm going to tell you
that if, upon arriving at my next ecstasy,
your big, warm hands
don't rescue me from this cold,
I can die without recourse.

Algún extraviado temblor

28

And nevertheless here I am.
Slipped into this scene of deaf clocks.
Perfectly distracted.
With a vague memory of horses set free in the wind.
With the vague premonition of death waiting on the corners.
I don't feel like pretending
sitting on my own tiled floor.
I'm still improvising
what I hardly intuit.
Also,
I have an inordinate capacity
for forgetting, suspecting, losing my bearings,
parceling myself out, getting lost and disorganizing everything.
That's why sometimes I wake up naked,

completamente amanecida.
Sin embargo,
cotidiana, madura y concienzudamente,
me dedico a tapar agujeros, remendar soledades.
A veces,
alcanzo a organizar mi desamparo,
vestir de números perfectos
mi gris melancolía.

Y sin embargo estoy aquí.
Sobrevenida.
No tengo ganas de ganar
la partida correcta y conveniente.

Me muero solamente
por aturdir sin prisa, delicadamente,
la quietud de una tarde de otoño,
desperdiciarme en un verso sencillo
y dormirme
sobre algún extraviado temblor de los sordos relojes.

Algún extraviado temblor

46

Cuánto es lo que valgo
así, cuando me quedo sola?
Cuánto pesa mi pobre dolor cuando sólo se quedan
estas cuatro paredes?
Qué más puedo perder?
A dónde puedo todavía escapar?
Cuánto puedo llorar todavía y para qué?
Así,
cuando mi sexo es una flor marchita
y hasta el verso se me muere en las manos,
cuando el amor es una historia absurda
y la palabra apenas, un papel en blanco,
cuánto valen mi pulso, mi temblor, mi ternura,
si soy sólo un pedazo de olvido
en medio del olvido.
Un día
voy a escapar de este presidio,
voy a arrancarme esta mordaza
voy a acabar con esta angustia.
Un día
voy a buscar el orgasmo de la muerte

completely ready for the day.
Nevertheless,
daily, maturely and conscientiously,
I am devoted to plugging holes and mending loneliness.
Sometimes,
I'm able to organize my helplessness,
and to dress my gray melancholy
in perfect numbers.

And nevertheless here I am.
Unexpectedly.
I don't feel like winning
the game correctly and conveniently.

I'm dying only
for having disturbed the quiet of an autumn afternoon,
slowly and delicately,
wasting my time on a simple verse
and falling asleep
upon some lost tremor of the deaf clocks.

Algún extraviado temblor

46

How much can I be worth
like this, when I'm alone?
How much does my grief weigh
when only these four walls remain?
What else can I lose?
Where can I still flee?
How much can I still cry and why?
So,
when my sex is a withered flower
and even a verse dies in my hands,
when love is an absurd history
and words are useless, a blank sheet of paper,
what's the value of my pulse, my tremor, my tenderness,
if I'm only a piece of oblivion
in the middle of oblivion.
One day
I'll escape from this prison,
I'll pull off this muzzle
I'll end this anguish.
One day
I'll search for the orgasm of death

que me salve definitivamente
de estas cuatro paredes,
de este papel en blanco,
de este saber
que los orgasmos se escapan
como el vuelo del sueño.

Un día,
voy a salir a rescatar
definitivamente lo que amo
detrás de la muerte.
Voy a salir a rescatar definitivamente el Sueño.

Algún extraviado temblor

—Y aquí se me va
esta hija mía . . .
Mis lágrimas
la bendicen.
Dice que va a lo que llaman Buenos Aires,
para algún trabajito;
con qué trabajo podrá esta muchacha inhábil.

—Esta, María,
se te va del todo
se nos va a perder,
a no regresar.
Quien va a Buenos Aires
cambia enteramente,
ya no conoce el Paraguay,
habla en otra forma,
y si acaso vuelve,
nos desprecia.

—Así no ha de ser,
no es bueno
que lo digas.
Ha de tornar
nuestra hija,
la de siempre.

Cuántos hijos nos llevaste,
Buenos Aires,
cuánto llanto nos dejaste,
cuánto sudor te has bebido.
Ya está bien,

that will save me decisively
from these four walls,
from this blank sheet of paper
from this knowledge
that orgasms escape
like the flight of dreams.

One day,
I'm going to rescue
decisively what I love
behind death.
I'm going out to rescue the Dream decisively

Algún extraviado temblor

—And here, this daughter of mine
is leaving me . . .
My tears
bless her.
She says she's going to what they call Buenos Aires,
for some little job;
what kind of job could this incompetent girl do?

—This one, María,
is leaving you behind forever,
we're going to lose her,
she'll never return.
Those who go to Buenos Aires
change completely,
they no longer know Paraguay,
they speak differently,
and if they do return,
they reject us.

—It shouldn't be that way,
it's not good
to say it.
Our daughter
has to return
just like she always was.

How many children, Buenos Aires,
have you taken away from us,
how many tears have you left us,
how much sweat have you imbibed?
All right then,

te has hartado:
te rogamos el retorno
de nuestros hijos.

Tesarái mboyve Antes del olvido

(Traducción al castellano del guaraní por Carlos Villagra Marsal
J.A. Rauskin y Susy Delgado)

3

Anoche soñé contigo.
Soñé que tú caminabas
sin saber que te miraba,
sin mirarme.
Soñé que yo te alcanzaba,
soñé que unía mis pies
a tus pies, y que mi cuerpo,
con el tuyo se enredaba.
Soñé que éramos dos niños,
dos en uno, un solo asombro
y una sola libertad,
caminando. . .

El patio de los duendes

8

Sobre todo, los sábados,
volver cabeceando hacia la tarde,
adormilada
de papeles y rostros y sudores
y montañas de horas
implacables, tiránicas.
Volver
hacia un extraño frío
que me toma las manos y recorre mi piel
palidecida al tiempo que la tarde.
Recobrar los contornos familiares
y deslizarme hacia el cansancio de las horas
de camisón y bañada de espera.
Y la espera me entornará los ojos
cuando la noche llegue de puntillas,
sembrando de suspiros,
las pequeñas colinas de mi pecho.
Y al paso de la noche,
me envolverá con un aliento de guitarras,

you've gotten your fill:
we beg you to return
our children.

Tesarái mboyve / Antes del olvido / Before Oblivion

(Translated to Spanish from Guaraní by Carlos Villagra Marsal, J.A. Rauskin, and Susy Delgado)

3

Last night I dreamt of you.
I dreamt that you were walking
without knowing that I watched you,
without looking at me.
I dreamt that I caught up to you,
I dreamt that I joined my feet
to your feet, and that my body
wrapped around yours.
I dreamt that we were two kids,
two in one, a single surprise
and a single liberty,
walking. . .

El patio de los duendes

8

Especially, on Saturdays,
returning and nodding off toward the afternoon,
half asleep
from papers, faces and sweat
and mountains of implacable,
tyrannical hours.
Returning
toward a strange cold
that takes my hands and runs over my skin,
paled in the afternoon.
Recovering the familiar surroundings
and slipping myself into the fatigue of the hours,
in a bathrobe and soaked in hope.
And the waiting will half close my eyes
when night arrives on tiptoes,
planting sighs
in the small knolls of my chest.
And as night passes,
it will wrap me up with a breath of guitars,

despertará una danza sensual en mi cintura,
vestirá de luceros mis hombros y caderas
y embriagará mi sexo con la miel de un recuerdo,
para amar lo que espera.
Amar absurdamente,
sobre todo, los sábados. . .

El patio de los duendes

6

La chamusquina del fuego
dejó sus huellas
en la memoria del niño.
Y la marca del fuego
me siguió en la vida.
Lo que no se borra,
bendición del fuego,
quemó entonces
mi palabra.

Tataypýpe / Junto al fuego

7

Humareda. . .
dispersándose
en los hondos recuerdos del niño.
Ya se apagó en mi memoria
el fuego viejo de aquel hogar.
Ya se asentaron y callaron
sus chisporroteos,
sus truenos,
su rumor.
Ya no está el lamido del fuego
allí donde estuvo el aliento de la lengua.

Tatapýpe / Junto al fuego

24

Largo ritual
de calentarse junto al fuego. . .
Que fuera apartando
despaciosamente
el frío y la noche.

it will awaken a sensual dance in my waist,
it will dress my shoulders and hips in stars
and it will enrapture my sex with the honey of a memory,
to love what awaits me.
To love absurdly,
especially on Saturdays.

El patio de los duendes

6

The fire singed
and left its marks
on the memory of the boy.
And the mark of the fire
followed me throughout life.
What was not erased
—a blessing of the fire—
then burned
my words.

Tataypýpe / Junto al fuego

7

cloud of smoke. . .
dispersing
in the deep memories of the boy.
The recollection of the old fire in that home
was extinguished in my memory.
Its spluttering,
crackling,
rustling
have become settled and quieted.
No longer is there the lick of the fire,
there, where the tongue's breath was.

Tatapýpe / Junto al fuego

24

A long ritual,
warming myself next to the fire . . .
It had slowly
pushed aside
the cold and the night.

Que me fue despertando
lentamente.
Largo calentarse
que desde lejos,
en el ensueño del olvido,
se enciende.
Rito del fuego
de otros tiempos,
lecho del recuerdo,
despierta y espanta
al olvido.

Tatapýpe Junto al fuego

12

Tal vez
porque hay un invierno
que me viene creciendo
muy adentro
desde hace mucho tiempo,
yo me quedé ese día
allá en el Sur,
en la playa lavada
por los vientos del mar.
Amarrada a sus altos eucaliptos,
a su aroma de invierno
que penetra hasta el alma,
aroma de eucalipto y caracoles,
de playa lavada por los vientos,
por el mar.

Sobre el beso del viento

14

Soy un país partido en dos,
recorrido en su parte más larga
por un agua profunda,
de vidas y de muertes
secretas.
Habita el sueño
mi región más huérfana,
frágil y, sin embargo, persistente,
sueño que se alimenta
tan sólo de mí mismo.

It awakened me
slowly.
A long gathering of warmth
that, from far away,
in the reverie of oblivion,
lit up.
A rite of fire
of other times,
a bed of memory,
awakens and frightens
oblivion.

Tatapýpe / Junto al fuego

12

Perhaps
because there is a winter
growing deeply
inside of me
for a long time,
I stayed that day
there in the South,
on the beach washed
by the sea's winds,
I was bound to the tall eucalyptus trees
to their winter aroma
that burrows into my soul,
an aroma of eucalyptus and snails,
of the beach washed by the winds,
by the sea.

Sobre el beso del viento

14

I am a country split into two,
along its length
runs a deep water
of secret
lives and deaths.
A dream inhabits
my most orphaned region,
fragile and, nevertheless, persistent,
a dream that is nurtured
only from within.

En la otra región se enseñorea
el dolor,
oxidado y aún fiero cuchillo,
que ha herido muchas carnes,
que se hace más cruel en cada herida.
Soy un país de sueño y de cuchillo.
Estoy partido en dos,
igual que mi destino.

Sobre el beso del viento

I

En un despertar
se pegó
a mi lengua,
estalló
en mi boca,
cosa insospechada,
el habla.
Cosa tiernísima,
buena de verdad,
aliento del cielo,
que nos da la vida
un momentito,
en medio de la noche.

Ayvu Membyre/ Hijo de aquel verbo

11

Si el amor siempre es
aquello no alcanzado,
con lo cual, soñaremos en vano, fundirnos,
¿quién fue el necio que habló de posesión?

Si aquello que se alcanza
ha empezado a morir,
por Dios, ¿a quién le importan
los amores posibles?

Las últimas hogueras

In the other region, suffering
takes possession,
a dagger, rusty but still terrifying,
that has wounded many bodies,
that becomes crueler with each wound.
I am a country of dreams and daggers.
I am split in two,
like my destiny.

Sobre el beso del viento

I

Once, upon awakening,
something unexpected
stuck
to my tongue,
exploded
in my mouth:
speech.
A very touching thing,
really good,
an encouragement from heaven
that gives us a moment
of life
in the dark of night.

Ayvu Membyre / Child of that Word

11

If love is always
what is unreachable,
what we dream about in vain
to join us together,
who is the fool who spoke about possession?

If what is reachable
has begun to die,
for God's sake, who cares
about possible loves?

Las últimas hogueras

OSCAR FERREIRO

TAPIR DE FUEGO

Del aire se descuelga
tamboreando el silencio
un gran tapir de fuego.

Galopa sobre el pico de las olas
deshecho todo cálculo
el gran tapir de fuego.

Suspendiendo las súplicas del agua
galopan los picachos de hielo y la tormenta
dos tapires de fuego.

Desquiciando los arcos de la tierra
destrozando las rutas de la fama
galopan incansables
tres tapires de fuego.

Cuatro caballos negros de Durero
a galope tendido
descubren las visiones desoladas
de Juan
de Juan de Patmos.

Antología (1982)

FONCIERE

Pasto rojo
sequía
y mi corazón reseco:
tizones crepitantes en la noche.
Sonora quemazón de aquellos años
y al fin aquella lluvia
misericordia y agua sobre el bosque
apagando rescoldos
con su luna crecida y su abundancia.

En los cerros de oriente
justa al Este
entre los troncos negros
la luz se reavivaba contra el cielo de cuarzo
y clamaban los monos

TAPIR OF FIRE

A great, fiery tapir
slips down from the air
drumming away the silence.

It gallops over the waves' crests,
every thought undone,
the great tapir of fire.

Suspending the pleas of the water,
galloping over stormy, icy mountain peaks,
two great tapirs of fire.

Disturbing the arcs of the land,
destroying the routes of fame,
untiring gallop
three tapirs of fire.

Four black horses of Dürer
at full gallop
reveal the desolate visions
of John
of John of Patmos.

Antología (1982)

FONCIERE

Red grass,
drought
and my heart wrung dry:
burning logs crackling in the night.
The intense, sonorous burning of those years
and finally that rain,
mercy and water upon the forest
smothering embers
with a full moon and its abundance.

In the eastern hills,
just to the east,
between the black tree trunks
the light renewed against the quartz sky
and the monkeys clamored

a una luna redonda de zapallos.

Sierra de Quince Puntas
denudada en cenizas y carbones
con mi congoja a solas.
Altos ríos en celo
con mil caballos muertos
desbordados
tremendos
y mil cuervos girando
sobre rojos espinos y arcoiris
para matar la estirpe de los hombres
para borrar las huellas de esta raza.

Antología (1982)

PASTORA MUERE EN LA TUMBA

Al poeta J. Antonio Bilbao

Pastora Céspedes, madre
madre ardiente y recelosa,
va a la guerra tras su hijo
pegada como una sombra.
Allá en el Chaco infernal
su fama el dolor pregona
y un negro pálpito en su alma
tiránico se le empoza,
Aunque camina con brío
ya presiente su derrota:
sólo está viendo en su espejo
a la infame burladora.

△

Y no le engañó el instinto,
pues, fue muy breve la historia:
apenas llega a Muñoz
su soldado se desploma
y ya las moscas tenaces
en sus heridas desovan.

△

— ¿Por qué, mi Dios, lo mataste?
¡maldita sea la hora!

to a round squash of a moon.

Sierra of Fifteen Peaks
denuded in ashes and charcoal
with my solitary anguish.
High rivers in heat
with a thousand dead horses
overflowing,
dreadful,
and a thousand crows spiraling
over red hawthorns and rainbows
to kill the lineage of man,
to wipe out all trace of this race.

Antología (1982)

PASTORA DIES ON THE TOMB

For the poet J. Antonio Bilbao

Pastora Céspedes, mother,
ardent and apprehensive mother,
follows her son to war,
sticking close like a shadow.
There, in the infernal Chaco,
her suffering spreads her renown,
and a dark murmur
settles tyrannically in her soul.
Though she walks with vigor
she foresees her defeat:
all she can see in her mirror
is the jesting scoundrel.

Δ

Her instinct didn't fail her,
well, the story was very brief:
hardly does her soldier arrive
at Muñoz when he swoons,
then tenacious flies
deposit eggs in his wounds.

Δ

"Why, oh God, did you kill him?
Damn this day!

Me han muerto mi único hijo
sin la ilusión de la gloria. . .
¿por qué, mi Dios, lo mataste?
¡Maldita sea la hora!
Pálido brotó inocente
de mi entraña pecadora. . .
¿Quiénes son los asesinos
que arman la guerra beoda?

Δ

—Aquí esperaré sentada
hasta que llegue la hora.

Δ

Pero han pasado veinte años. . .
y en vano el milagro imploras.
¡Grandes se han vuelto tus ojos
de escudriñar en las sombras!
El salitral de la muerte
hurgan hambrientas las zorras
y tú, sentada en la tumba,
triste madre cimarrona,
en vano el milagro esperas:
la inmensidad está sorda.
¡Pobre loca, si es más fácil
que aceite te den las rocas!
El mundo ya lo ha olvidado
y sólo el viento lo nombra
cuando en las abras heladas
la muerta luna tramonta:
o cuando un lánguido leste
estremece las totoras.
Negra y larga es la tu pena,
llorando triste y tan sola,
tu negra pena enredada
de un triste sauce en la copa.
Y qué largas son las trenzas
con que, locamente, escobas
y—con lágrimas saladas—
riegas el suelo de tosca.

Δ

Déjale en paz a tu muerto,
calle tu voz quejumbrosa:

They've killed my only son
without any hope of glory. . .
Why, oh God, did you kill him?
Damn this day!
Pale and innocent, he sprang
from my sinful womb. . .
Who are the murderers
that started this drunken war?"

Δ

"I'll sit right here and wait
until the time comes."

Δ

But twenty years have passed. . .
and in vain you implore a miracle.
Your eyes have grown so large
from squinting in the shadows!
The saltpeter bed of death
is rummaged by hungry foxes
and you, seated on the tomb,
sad, fugitive mother,
you wait in vain for the miracle:
the universe is deaf.
Poor, mad woman, it's easier to
squeeze oil from rocks!
The world has already forgotten him
and only the wind names him
when, in the frozen valleys,
the dead moon sinks behind the mountains:
or when a languid east wind
rattles the cattails.
Long and black is your suffering,
crying so sadly and alone,
your dark pain is wound
around the top of a willow.
And how long are the braids
you madly use as a broom
and—with salty tears—
you irrigate the land of tufa.

Δ

Leave your dearly deceased in peace,
quiet your plaintive voice:

cien mil guerreros se han ido
y a nadie volver le toca.
Oscuro sueño de plomo
aplasta a pilas y collas.
Sólo en el campo desierto
vaga la paz sin zozobras:
la vieja tierra vengada
oscuramente se goza.
(Untuosos dedos de polvo
palpan ásperas escorias).

Δ

La eterna muerte otra vez
forjó una clara victoria
y en los campos de batalla
insomnes vagan los poras.

Δ

—¿Qué buscas, mamá, a estas hora?
—A quién sino a vos, mi hijito,
que sin piedad me abandonas,
—No puedo moverme, madre,
es muy estrecha mi fosa
y un sueño de plomo extraño
noche y día me devora.
—Despertate, que amanece. . .
la madrugada está rosa y el viento fresco disputa
al paloverde su aroma.
—Sí, mamá, celeste y rosa,
la aurora es, celeste y rosa:
pero también es amarga,
amarga como achicoria.
—Levantate que los pájaros
no sé si cantan o lloran:
pero el dolor de la vida
disimulan o pregonan.
—Ah, si pudiera salir. . .!
me comería amapolas
o me pondría a mascar
un puño de cal y coca.
—Pero este día es hermoso;
sonríe como una novia;
los venadillos de campo
alegremente retozan.
—Ay, mamá, no me molestes,

a hundred thousand warriors have gone
and no one can return.
A dark, leaden dream,
smashes Paraguayans and Bolivians.
Only in the wide desert
can peace wander without worry:
the old land, now avenged,
mysteriously rejoices.
(Oily, dusty fingers
touch the harsh dross.)

Δ

Eternal death again
forged a clear victory
and in the battlegrounds
the ghosts roam sleeplessly.

Δ

"What are you looking for, mother, this time?"
"What else, but you, my little boy,
who abandoned me without any pity."
"I can't move, mother,
my grave is very narrow
and a strange, leaden sleep
devours me night and day."
"Wake up, the sun is coming out. . .
the early morning is pink
and the fresh wind contends with
the paloverde for its aroma."
"Yes, mother, celestial and pink,
the dawn is celestial and pink:
but it's also bitter,
bitter like chicory."
"Get up; I don't know if the birds
are singing or crying:
they're either concealing or proclaiming
the suffering of life."
"Oh, if I were able to get out. . .!
I'd eat the poppies
or I'd set about chewing
a handful of limestone and coca leaves."*
"But today is beautiful:
smile like a bride:
the little deer romp
merrily in the country."
"Oh, mother, don't bother me,

porque la muerte es mi esposa
y esta sed de eternidad
sólo la sacio en su copa.
—Está bien: pero a tu lado. . .
¡cuánto me aterra estar sola!
Esperaré noche y día
hasta que ustedes me acojan.
—Déjame en paz, madre amada,
que la muerte está celosa. . .
igual volverá a acostarme
bajo el plomo de una losa.

*Un trozo de cal y un puño de hojas de coca al masticarse producen un leve efecto narcótico.

El gallo de la alquería

LA GUARDIA URBANA

—Por vos, mi pobre inocente,
vendrá un día la montada. . .
—La montada ya no existe;
no empieces con tus macanas.
—Da lo mismo, ya me acuerdo,
le dicen la guardia urbana
pero igual, a garrotazos,
harán charque de tu espalda.
A arrancarte de este rancho
un día vendrán sin falta.
—Yo les daré un buendía
con este cabo de nácar.
—No te hagas ilusiones.
No te servirán de nada,
hijo mío, esas sonseras
que en la cabeza te bailan!
—No es cierto, mamá, en el mundo
la nueva idea está en marcha.
—Soy una pobre burrera
con mi burro y mi burjaca.
La banda es para los ricos,
para los pobres la guacha.
Soy una triste burrera
bebiendo en jarro de lata
las lágrimas de mi gente
y las mías más amargas!

Δ

because death is my bride
and this thirst for eternity
I can only satisfy with her wine glass."
"All right: but at your side. . .
how terrified I am to be alone!
I'll wait night and day
until you all come for me."
"Leave me in peace, dear mother,
because death is jealous. . .
she'll return to put me back again
under the lead of a gravestone."

*A piece of limestone and a wad of coca leaves, when chewed together produce a mild narcotic effect.

El gallo de la alquería

THE URBAN GUARD

"You're so naïve, one day
the cavalry will come for you. . ."
"The cavalry no longer exists;
don't start with your nonsense."
"It's the same thing, I remember,
now they call it the 'urban guard,'
but they're the same, with their cudgels
they'll make jerky out of your back.
Get going out of this ranch,
one day they'll come, for sure."
"I'll give them their good morning
with this nacre gun butt."
"You're dreaming.
Those silly notions
dancing in your head, my boy,
won't get you anywhere."
"That's not true, mother, there's a new
way of thinking now in the world."
"I'm a poor donkey driver
with my donkey and my pilgrim's bag.
The band is for the rich,
the whip for the poor.
I'm just a donkey driver
drinking my people's tears
out of a tin jug
and mine are the bitterest."

Δ

Desde Ysaty hasta Asunción
es larga la caminata
y a punta de bayoneta
resulta mucho más larga.
Maniatado con alambre
y a empellones de culatas
desde Ysaty, por Dos Bocas,
lo repunta la canalla.

Δ

—Un rojo pañuelo al cuello
será el premio a tus pureadas;
pero no será de trapo
sino de sangre barata.*

Δ

Sobre el óleo de los charcos
patinan las carcajadas
y un pípuu alcohólico y largo
se clava en La Salamanca.
Un degüello de yuyales
asustado el viento ensaya
y ganan los albañales
rápidamente las ratas.
Como un cíclope mareado
un tuerto el ojo se palpa
y los horrores del mundo
tan increíbles repasa.
Asunción, sucia y artera,
sin azahares, sin nada,
que no sea la insolencia
de tus cobardes mesnadas.

Δ

—Suéltenme las manos, perros,
y así sabrán quién les habla!
Ese trapo colorado
les meteré en la garganta!

Δ

*El pañuelo rojo era símbolo de los partidarios de los Colorados.

From Ysaty to Asunción
it's a long walk
and it's even longer
when escorted by a bayonet
Hands tied with wire
and pushed along with rifle butts
from Ysaty, through Dos Bocas,
the swine pushed him forward.

Δ

"A red kerchief around your neck
will be your reward for your showing off;
but it won't be of red cloth,
only cheap blood."*

Δ

Bellows of laughter skate
on the oily surface of the puddles
and a long, drunken shout
pierces through La Salamanca bar.
A frightened wind attempts
a beheading of a clump of weeds,
and the rats quickly
get to the sewers.
Like a drunken Cyclops,
a one-eyed man feels his eye
and reviews the incredible
horrors of the world.
Asunción, dirty and cunning,
without orange blossoms, or anything
other than the insolence
of your cowardly armed soldiers.

Δ

"Free my hands, you dogs,
and then you'll know who's talking to you!
I'll stick that red bandanna
down your throats."

Δ

*The red kerchief was the symbol of the followers of the Colorados.

—Emboty nde picha'ï.
Re ñemboayúra pytäta.
—Dios te salve y tu abogado,
ápente ya reikopáma. . . *

El gallo de la alquería

* —Deja de lado la miseria
y ponte un pañuelo colorado.
—Dios te salve y tu abogado,
aquí contigo ya se acaba.

—Emboty nde picha'ï.
Re ñemboayúra pytäta.
—Dios te salve y tu abogado,
ápente ya reikopáma. . . *

El gallo de la alquería

* "Just set aside your misery
and put on the Colorado bandanna."
"May God save you and your counsel,
it's all over for you here."

RENÉE FERRER

CARAMAÑOLA

Puñado de latón donde palpita
un recuerdo de siesta
en alucinada vastedad.

Manantial prisionero
alivianando el tajo del insomnio
en el solazo
con la fría moldura de sus labios.

Su roce se recuesta
con esa mansedumbre de pausa acostumbrada
sobre la celda del cansancio.

Compañera febril
cuando la piel acampa
bajo un astro de arenas azuladas.

Mujer para un orgasmo interminable
cediendo brevemente sus honduras
en los claros del alba.

Se inclinan sus sorbos torrenciales
a regar un desierto de amapolas abiertas.

Y estéril ya su lecho de vendimia,
el secreto remanso de su cauce,
se queda, compasiva,
recogiendo caricias en la noche
bajo un cielo de estrellas ateridas.

Desde el cañadón de la memoria

CÁNTARO

Redondez perfumada
de tierra recocida
con un plato en la boca
y un jarro del revés.

En capullo de barro
queda el agua dormida,
aprisionada y limpia

CANTEEN

A fistful of tin where a memory
of the siesta palpitates
in the hallucinated, vast expanse.

A captive spring
alleviating the slash of insomnia
in the blazing sun
with the cold molding of its lips.

Its contact reclines
with the gentleness of an accustomed pause
over the prison of fatigue.

A restless companion
when the skin camps down
below a star of bluish sands.

A woman for an interminable orgasm,
briefly ceding her depths
at the early light of dawn.

Her torrential sips incline
to irrigate a desert of open poppies.

Now sterile the bed of her vintage,
the secret backwater of her river bed
remains, sympathetic,
gathering caresses in the night
under a sky numbed with cold.

Desde el cañadón de la memoria

WATER PITCHER

Perfumed roundness
of hardbaked soil
with a plate in its mouth
and an inverted jug.

In the clay bud
the water remains asleep,
imprisoned and clean

para mi ávida sed.

Que modestia tostada
la de tu curva uncida
por dos manos morenas
teñidas de tu tez.

Cántaro que retienes
en telúrico seno
un sabor de agua mansa
con sobria sencillez.

Entre mis labios canta
tu líquida frescura,
el límpido sonido
de tanta redondez.

Campo y cielo

VIII

Acurrucado y solo,
jinete de la brisa
hacia la orilla del mar.
Empaparse de sal. Sentir la espuma,
el siseo desarmado de la espuma.
El sol reverberando
en el bolsón de los cerros.

Cautivar el instante fugitivo
en la retina de un adiós
que permanece,
y aspirar
salitre, canto, brisa marinera.

Calado de abandono
en las espaldas del viento junto al mar.
Retener esa curva de luna
recién nacida.
El blanco cementerio de la espuma.
Sobre conchas quebradas
estampar una huella lineal.

Cuerpos
tendidos, libres, invitantes.
Párpados entornados,

for my avid thirst.

What toasted modesty
is your curve, plotted
by two brown hands
tinted by your skin.

You, pitcher, that retains
in your earthly bosom
a taste of gentle water
with sober simplicity.

Between my lips sings
your liquid freshness,
the limpid sound
of so much roundness.

Campo y cielo

VIII

Huddled up and alone,
he rides on the breeze
toward the seashore.
Soaking in seawater. Feeling the foam,
the dismantled hiss of the foam.
The sun reverberating
in the pocket of the hills.

Capturing the fleeting instant
in the retina of a goodbye
that remains,
and to inhale
saltpeter, song, sea breezes.

Soaked through with abandon
on the wind's back, next to the sea.
Preserving that curve
of the new moon.
The white cemetery of the foam.
Stamping down a straight track
over crushed shells.

Bodies
stretched out, free, seductive.
Eyelids half-closed,

entrega a voces.
Mentes
como sábanas blancas desprendidas.

Noche.
Noche y luna.
Y ese rumor de caracolas
en la arena.
Manos asidas. Pasos. Besos.
Ya se desnuda el sol
Es el alba.

La espuma entristece cada ola.
Peces hinchados flotan en sus crestas.
Acurrucado y solo
solloza sobre el viento
abandonado del mar.

Sobreviviente

XIII

a Hugo Rodríguez-Alcalá

La inteligencia en una hoguera
fue vencida.
Ardieron la belleza,
la palabra,
el sonido.
Con dolor se aprenderá todo
nuevamente
en otro mundo errático y vacío.

El ingenio del hombre tiene gusto a ceniza.
Computadoras, técnica, artefactos,
máquinas que ayudaban a hablarnos desde lejos,
a escribir un deseo en otras latitudes,
son ceniza en el aire enajenado,
cenizas los colores y la forma,
el andamio de notas y silencios,
el verbo, el pensamiento.

El hombre ha transformado
piedra en luces,
estiércol en semilla,
arena en beso.

a shouting surrender.
Minds
like white sheets thrown asunder.

Night.
Night and moon.
And that murmur of sea conches
in the sand.
Hands interlaced. Steps. Kisses.
Already the sun undresses.
It is dawn.

Foam saddens each wave.
Swollen fish float on their crests.
Huddled up and alone
he sobs upon the wind,
abandoned by the sea.

Sobreviviente (*Survivor*)

XIII

to Hugo Rodríguez-Alcalá

Intelligence was defeated
in a bonfire.
Beauty,
words,
sounds, they burned it all.
Painfully, everything will be learned
once again
in another erratic and empty world.

The genius of man savors ashes.
Computers, technologies, artifacts,
machines that helped us talk with others from afar,
or write a wish in other latitudes,
all are ashes in the alienated air,
color and form now ashes,
the scaffolding of notes and pauses,
language, thought.

Man has transformed
rock into lights,
manure into seed,
sand into kisses.

Todo sabe a cenizas, a cenizas.

Respira aún la tierra su diferencia de horas,
pero nadie lo nota.
No hay albas retrasadas a la noche ligera,
sólo un sabor de ausencia
cuando lloran los pájaros
el duelo de su voz.

Sobreviviente

TRÍPTICO DE LOS ENIGMAS
TRANSMIGRACIÓN

Nocturno N° 7 de Chopin

Vengo del lugar donde se abren
los misterios promisorios del alma;
del valle original de los destinos.

Vengo del lugar donde germinan
el pulso y la palabra.

De ese espacio primigenio partí
para llegar
hasta la cima o el abismo
del desvelo.

Guardo el secreto designio de transitar
los inconexos mundos que me habitan,
los múltiples rostros olvidados.

A través de otros cuerpos peregriné
largamente
para amar,
cincelando mis ansias,
los misteriosos recovecos del ser.
Llevo el andamio de la luz
en mi corazón
para pulir las aristas inconclusas
de mi alma.

Soy ansia y carne,
eco, latido,
canto, tristeza,
voluntad, fuego,
amor y sueño.

It all tastes of ash, of ash.

The earth still breathes its difference of hours,
but nobody notices.
For the swift night, there are no delayed dawns,
only a taste of absence
when the birds mourn
the grief of their voice.

Sobreviviente (Survivor)

TRYPTYCH OF THE ENIGMAS
TRANSMIGRATION

Nocturne Nº 7 by Chopin

I come from the place where
promising mysteries of the soul are opened;
of the original valley of destinies.

I come from the place where
the pulse and the word originate.

From that original place I departed
to get to
the peak or the abysm
of sleeplessness.

I keep the secret plan for commuting
through the unconnected worlds that live within me,
the multiple forgotten faces.

Through other bodies I wandered
for a long time
to love,
chiseling my anxieties,
the mysterious twists and turns of being.
I carry the scaffolding of light
in my heart
to polish the unfinished edges
of my soul.
I am anxiety and flesh,
echo, pulse,
song, sadness,
will, fire,
love and dream.

Soy carne y agua,
ahinco, anhelo,
elipse alada estrenando sueños
en las praderas del universo,

en las honduras del universo.

Soy sangre y pulso,
camino, viento,
corriente abrupta,
remanso entero
flecha y distancia
sobre la huella puntual del péndulo.
Jirón y herida de amanecidos sueños
pasión de andar errante,
impenitente,
congoja de latir
y siembra alegre,
navío, timonel
y espuma suelta,
desaliento, dolor,
vuelo resuelto.

Certeza de que la muerte
no se nombra,
y la tumba es portal
y otra vez sueño.

Vuelvo adonde despuntan
los brotes encendidos del alma;
al valle donde se acuñan los desvelos;
allí donde todo se contagia de manantial.

Vuelvo al recinto de la luz,
embriagada de verbo y transparencia,
a cubrirme la frente de absoluto.

¡Oh plenitud
de retornar
sin vestiduras
a ese lugar;
siendo otra vez
toda de luz,
diáfana,
libre,
inmaterial.

I am of flesh and water,
zeal, desire,
a winged ellipse, trying out dreams
in the prairies of the universe,

in the depths of the universe.

I am blood and pulse,
path, wind,
abrupt current,
an entire pool,
arrow and distance
on the punctual path of the pendulum.
A shred and a wound of daybreak dreams,
a passion for wandering aimlessly,
unrepentantly,
palpitation anxiety
and a merry time for sowing,
ship, rudder
and scattered foam,
discouragement, suffering,
a flight resolved.

A certainty that death
is not named,
and the tomb is a gate
and once again a dream.

I return to where they cut off
the illuminated buds of the soul:
to the valley where they coin sleepless nights;
there, where everything is touched by spring water.

I return to the abode of light,
enraptured with the verb and the transparency,
to cover my forehead with the absolute.

Oh, the plenitude
of returning
without clothing
to that place;
once again being
all light,
diaphanous,
free,
immaterial.

Alma
    ataviada
        de universo.

Nocturnos

ANDINISMO

Los labios suben;
laboriosos, escalan las uñas,
las rodillas
—andinistas de fuego—,
ávidos, se demoran en los pozos de sombra
que conceden la luz.
La exploración se adentra
entre el follaje hirsuto y la fuente pequeña.
Se someten al hueso de un codo guerrillero,
a la remota axila,
a la nuca en declive;
hacen alto en las manos,
manantial de arcanas vibraciones.
La lengua los retiene
en el desfiladero que aísla los pezones,
morados promontorios que erguidamente gimen.
Poderosos ascienden el risco del latido,
la inminencia de amar,
el tembloroso aliento de las cumbres sedientas.
Lentos, suben los labios
hacia el santurario del deseo,
hasta la sonrosada quemazón que los espera.

Itinerario del deseo

LAS CAJAS

Bajo la lámpara
tengo un rebaño de cajas,
pequeños cubos,
cierre
y bisagras;
pastorean la luz
sobre el vidrio
y yo, sin saber qué hacer,
lustro sus tapas.
La mudéjar
la compré

A soul
    adorned
        with the universe.

Nocturnos

CLIMBING THE ANDES

The lips move up;
laboriously, they scale the toenails,
the knees
—mountain climbers of fire—
avidly, they dally in the shadowy pools
that admit the light.
The exploration goes deeper
into the thick foliage and the small spring.
They yield to the bone of a guerrilla elbow,
to the remote underarm,
to the sloping nape of the neck,
they make a stop at the hands,
a spring of arcane vibrations.
The tongue retains them
in the narrow path that separates the nipples,
purple promontories that sigh erectly.
Powerfully, they ascend the cliff of the pulsation,
the imminence of loving,
the trembling breath of the thirsty peaks.
Slowly, the lips climb
toward the sanctuary of desire,
up to the blushing blaze that awaits them.

Itinerario del deseo

THE BOXES

Under the lamp
I have a heard of boxes,
little cubes,
clasps,
hinges;
they graze on the light
on the glass
and I, not knowing what to do,
polish their tops.
The Moorish one
I bought

en una subasta;
era en París
y llovía;
Vallejo se aproximó
y por poco lo seguí,
encandilada,
del brazo;
me retuvo aquella caja
que hubiera querido darte
para esconder algo,
no sé,
algún deseo
en su diminuto espacio;
en el pastillero esmaltado
acomodé tu sonrisa,
la misma
que aquella tarde
se resbaló
de tus labios;
en la de Limoges,
los reproches,
en la de cristal,
mis ansias,
en la de nácar
—cuidado—
que la atoré de palabras,
las que callé en la vigilia,
las que entresueños
me hablabas;
las que no eran para mí,
en el monedero de plata,
—aguijones de tu voz—,
ésas
no quiero escucharlas;
qué raudales de silencio
retuvieron
esas cajas.
Ahora,
ya están vacías;
que no se le ocurra
a nadie
abrirlas:
no tienen nada.

Itinerario del deseo

at an auction:
it was in Paris
and it was raining;
Vallejo approached
and I almost followed him,
dazzled,
on his arm;
that box held me back,
the one I had wanted to give you
to hide something,
I don't know,
some wish
in its tiny space;
in the little lacquered tablet box
I made a place for your smile,
the same one
that on that afternoon
slipped
from your lips;
in the one from Limoges,
I put the reproaches,
in the glass one,
my yearnings,
in the one of mother-of-pearl
—careful—
that I clogged with words
those I kept to myself during my sleeplessness,
those you murmured to me
in your half-sleep;
the words not intended for me,
in the silver money purse
—sharp goads of your voice—
those words
I don't want to hear them;
what torrents of silence
those boxes
retained.
Now,
now they're empty;
nobody
better think about
opening them;
there's nothing inside.

Itinerario del deseo

LOS ROCES

De unos roces a esta parte,
entre la luminosidad de verte
y la desdicha de que te me pierdas
tras el amasijo de las consideraciones
y los péndulos tiránicos
y la nunca bien ponderada costumbre
de la rotulación estéril,
mientras desfallece la carne
de tantos orgasmos inventados
como fantasmas con tu rostro
y sin ninguna esperanza,
languidecen las miradas,
se indiferencian;
ni qué decir de las fogatas
que devoraban nuestros ojos,
y cómo sabíamos evitarlo
eso de rozarnos sin darnos cuenta,
o tal vez
ni siquiera rozarnos,
sabiendo
que los pecados de la postergación
son los más graves.

El ocaso del milenio

IV [fragmentos]

ocho fantasmas
están de salida
                    ¿no los ves?
. . .
                    seguro que
                    los ves
ocho ánimas
deambulan sin premura
ni piedras
en las manos
siguiendo un derrotero
que el olvido mancilla

                    ¿acaso no
                    las ves?

desde el campanario

FRICTIONS

A few frictions ago,
between the afterglow of seeing you
and the misfortune of your losing me
after the mess of all the considerations
and the tyrannical pendulums
and the never well-thought-out custom
of sterile labeling,
while our flesh weakens
from so many fake orgasms
like ghosts with your face
and with no hope,
our glances languish,
become indifferent;
nothing more to say about the bonfires
that devoured our eyes,
nor how we learned to avoid it,
rubbing each other the wrong way
without even realizing it,
or perhaps
not even bothering one other,
knowing
that the sins of postponement
are the most serious.

El ocaso del milenio

IV [fragments]

eight ghosts
are on their way out
                    don't you see them?
. . .
                    of course
                    you see them
eight souls
wandering without haste
nor stones
in their hands
following a route
that oblivion will blemish
                    you really
                    don't see them?

from the bell tower

de la Catedral
donde pernocta el tiempo
las manecillas de un reloj
con arritmia incurable
observan pensativas
unas sombras
ni siquiera ya sombras
que atraviesan el viento
sin tocarlo
en tanto un gorrión
repara sorprendido
que en las alas le tiembla
un gusto de agonía
. . .
con pasos sólo audibles
en la estación del sueño
ocho fantasmas
remontan los rojos escalones
masticando un resabio
de coraje ultrajado.
¿en la furtiva penumbra
no se ven?

*Las cruces del olvido**

*Los poemas de este libro reflejan los acontecimientos del "marzo paraguayo" de 1999, en el cual varios manifestantes—en protesta contra el asesinato del vicepresidente, Luis María Argaña y en apoyo al presidente Raúl Cubas Grau—fueron acribillados y muertos por francotiradores de la oposición a su gobierno.

of the cathedral
where time spends the night
the hands of the clock
with an incurable arrhythmia
pensively observe
some shadows
not even shadows any longer
that cross the wind
without touching it
while a sparrow
notices with surprise
that its wings tremble
with a taste of agony
. . .
with steps audible only
in the season of dreams
eight ghosts
climb the red steps
chewing on the aftertaste
of an outraged anger.
in the furtive penumbra
can't you see them?

*Las cruces del olvido**

*The poems in this book reflect the events of the "marzo paraguayo" (Paraguayan March) of 1999. A number of demonstrators—protesting the assassination of Vice President Luis María Argaña, and supporting incumbent President Raúl Cubas Grau—were shot and killed by snipers of the opposition to his government.

JOAQUÍN MORALES

NATURALEZA MUERTA, 1

No las perdices de ojos
probablemente reventados
ni el racimo de sus patas
confundiéndose con las hierbas aromáticas;
tampoco el vaso de barro
que muestra claramente
las huellas de los dedos que lo moldearon;
ni siquiera las oscuras
tablas irregulares de la mesa,
vetas y nudos guardando para sí
el olor del bosque todavía:

no el viejo tema de apariencia y realidad,
ni el del tiempo remansado en pinceladas
que la memoria vivifica y recompone:

quizá —aunque es casi imposible la certeza—
quizás la total aprehensión
de un reflejo amarillo en un pequeño pico pardo.

Postales de Bizancio

SOBRE LA MORTANDAD EN LAS RUTAS

And then went down to the ship . . .

Y entonces bajamos hasta el auto
rumbo a la autopista sur
dejando el barrio todavía dormido,
sombras a cada vuelta,
sombras cada uno junto al otro,
entrando en la corriente de luces y carteles,
ramalazos de viento en la autopista,
neón parpadeante y señales inscritas
en alguna región de lo percibido,
siempre más rápido,
en los sentidos apenas un rasguño,
contracciones de una membrana
que aglutina las cosas,
un murmullo anónimo que conduce
al hueco de un silencio y un bostezo,
quizás ese alguien que al partir amábamos

STILL LIFE, I

It's not the partridges with their eyes
probably bursting out,
nor the bouquet of their legs
mingled with aromatic herbs;
nor the clay vase
that clearly shows
the prints of the fingers that molded it;
not even the dark,
irregular boards of the table,
whose veins and nodules still retain
the aroma of the forest:

not the old theme of appearance and reality,
nor the one of time briefly detained in brush strokes
that memory vivifies and recomposes:

perhaps—though certainty is almost impossible—
perhaps it's the complete apprehension
of a yellow reflection in a small dark beak.

Postales de Bizancio

ABOUT THE DEATH TOLL ON HIGHWAYS

And then went down to the ship...

And then we went down to the car
on the way to the southbound highway,
leaving behind the still-sleeping neighborhood,
shadows everywhere,
shadows, each one beside another,
entering the current of lights and signs,
lashes of wind on the highway,
blinking neon and signals inscribed
on some region of what can be perceived,
more and more quickly,
hardly a scratch on the senses,
contractions of a membrane
that agglutinates things,
an anonymous murmur that leads to
the void of a silence and a yawn,
perhaps that someone we loved when we departed

y ahora es una cara horriblemente iluminada
por luces alternativamente rojas y verdes,
y la radio que sólo capta ruidos,
pedazos de frases en extraños idiomas,
una canción, de hombre o de mujer la voz, y una flauta,
antiguos contornos y cadencias
que están por revelarte algo
pero alguien pregunta qué hora es,
y cuánto falta,
y qué eran esas como torres que recién pasamos,
y la discusión de que no,
son árboles agrandados por la neblina,
tampoco,
chimeneas de una fábrica en construcción,
tampoco,
las columnas de un templo en ruinas,
tampoco,
y tratas de recordar
qué fue exactamente lo que viste
y qué te habían advertido que verías,
y se te escapa el contorno preciso,
imposible amoldarlo a ese ordenamiento previo,
viento cruzado y extraños diseños de las estrellas
mezclados a la sensación de velocidad,
todo eso excediendo los modelos,
e intentas construir algo nuevo
que la musiquita no te deja completar
—estorbando, acechando, rondando—
un nuevo concepto,
una nueva palabra
que comprima y deseche la confusión,
pero sólo te resultan claros
los carteles fosforescentes,
flechas y curvas y números,
y prohibiciones que, acatadas,
nos deberían proteger
según nos prometieron
entre abrazos de despedida y un poco de llanto
(pero sólo un poco),
y terminas por dudar haber visto las ruinas,
haber escuchado la pregunta,
haber sentido en la cara el golpe del viento,
y lo único seguro, lo indudable,
son las flechas y números y curvas,
ni siquiera la canción,
ni siquiera el movimiento, ni siquiera esos faros

and now there's a face horribly illuminated
by lights alternately red and green,
and the radio only pulls in noises,
fragments of phrases in strange languages,
a song, with a man's or a woman's voice, a flute,
very old contours and cadences
that are about to reveal something to you
but someone asks what time it is
and how much longer to go,
and what were those tower-like things we just passed,
and the discussion that no,
they are trees enlarged by the fog,
not that either,
chimneys of a factory under construction,
not that either,
the columns of a temple in ruins,
not that either,
and you try to remember
what it was exactly you saw
and what they had warned you would see,
and the precise outline escapes you,
impossible to mold it into that previous ordering,
a crosswind and strange designs of the stars
mixed with the sensation of speed,
all of this exceeding the models,
and you try to construct something new,
something music will not let you complete
—bothering, lying in wait, hovering—
a new concept,
a new word
that compresses and casts confusion aside,
but only the phosphorescent signs
seem clear to you,
arrows and curves and numbers,
and warnings that, if obeyed,
should protect us
like they promised us
during the farewell hugs and a bit of crying
(but only a little),
and you wind up doubting you've seen the ruins,
having listened to the question,
having felt the slap of the wind in your face,
and the only thing for sure, the unquestionable thing,
are the arrows and numbers and curves,
not even the song,
not even the movement, not even those headlights

súbitamente en sentido contrario,
encandilando,
y el único recurso de desviar
pero ya es tarde:
así es que finalmente llegamos
al lugar predicho por Circe
(en quien tampoco creías)
pero ninguno se da cuenta,
todos los sentidos perdiendo sustancia
a través de las fisuras.

Postales de Bizancio

CONTRA LAS PALABRAS

He crecido dispuesto
a lo semejante y lo contiguo,
a todo lo que no es yo,
pero así supone cada uno;
y no me importa que yo y cada uno,
lo contiguo y lo semejante
seamos juntos una querida escayola:
palabras, meras palabras,
fraguado polvo de ruido
para proteger un hueso roto o en exceso blando,
modelar la carne que nos crece, terca,
como hiedra sobre muro derruido,
y hospedar al gusano hereditario,
residuo de la estrella que perdimos.
Tampoco yo lo entiendo:
la metáfora es un vicio,
garganta y lengua son mucho para mí,
y estas palabras se me mezclan y confunden
como las caras esquivas de una muchedumbre.
Y esta confusión, sinceramente,
me preocupa:
pero la ordenación de las cosas
es insulto a cada una
si el pegarles rótulos
y barajarlos con cuidado
nos deja en las vitrinas un olor rancio,
sequedad de pergamino.
¿Cómo puedo atreverme entonces a escribir
'Yo he visto el relámpago'
'Yo he amado como nadie'?

suddenly coming right at you,
blinding,
and your only recourse is to swerve,
but it's too late:
so, finally we arrive
at the place predicted by Circe
(whom you didn't believe in either)
but no one realizes,
all the senses lose their substance
through the fissures.

Postales de Bizancio

AGAINST WORDS

I have grown up prepared
for what is similar and nearby,
for all that is not myself,
but that's what everyone supposes;
and I don't care if I and everyone,
if what is near and what is similar,
form together a precious plaster cast,
words, mere words,
dust forged of noise
to protect a bone, broken or excessively soft,
to mould flesh that grows on us, tenaciously,
like ivy on a demolished wall,
and to host the hereditary worm,
residue of the star that we missed.
I don't understand it either:
metaphors are a vice,
the throat and the tongue are a lot for me,
and these words get me mixed up and confused
like the evasive faces of a crowd.
And this confusion sincerely
worries me:
but the ordination of things
is an insult to every one of them
if labeling
and shuffling them carefully
leaves us a rancid odor on the showcases
the dryness of parchment.
How can I then dare write
"I have seen the lightning"
"Nobody has loved like I have?"

Sucede que todos hablan así con todos,
y confieso que yo también.
Palabras, meras palabras,
Tampoco yo lo entiendo.

Postales de Bizancio

ARTE POETICA, 1

Palabras de papel,
palabras de viento.
Se van, se pierden,
se olvidan,
no sirven para nada
y no dan de comer.

Postales de Bizancio

ARTE POETICA 3

El completo asco a las palabras
es la primera gracia del estilo.
Porque el corazón del poema
está en el lado izquierdo del silencio,
como en el hombre.
Y a veces el poema es un silencio largo
—como el hombre mismo.

Postales de Bizancio

POLIEDRO DE LA MELANCOLÍA

Por cuántas caras difundes,
poliedro,
la suave melancolía que te envuelve.
Con cuántas aristas cortas
las miradas que quieren estudiarte.
Por cuáles grietas se escapa
tu tranquilo tiempo
que a los dedos del artesano manchan.
Quién conoce tus dorsos
Por qué se te asignó esa perspectiva
Qué rigurosa deformidad escondes
o quieres revelar y es imposible
Qué artífice mágico te salvará
reordenando tus múltiples rostros

It's just that everyone speaks this way to one another,
and I confess I do too.
Words, mere words,
I don't understand it either.

Postales de Bizancio

THE ART OF POETRY, 1

Words of paper,
words of wind.
They go away, they get lost,
they get forgotten,
they're no good for anything
and they don't feed you.

Postales de Bizancio

THE ART OF POETRY, 3

The complete disgust for words
is the first grace of style.
Because the heart of the poem
is on the left side of silence,
as it is in man.
And at times the poem is a long silence
—like man himself.

Postales de Bizancio

POLYHEDRON OF MELANCHOLY

Through how many faces do you disseminate,
polyhedron,
the soft melancholy that envelopes you?
With how many edges do you cut off
the stares that want to study you?
Through what cracks
does your peaceful time escape
and stain the fingers of the artisan?
Who knows your backsides?
Why was that perspective assigned to you?
What severe deformity do you hide
or wish to reveal, though it's impossible?
What magic trick will save you
as you rearrange your multiple faces?

Cuál sabia hipótesis, cuál geometría
tu duración contienen, y tu espacio
Qué músico maestro
tus números en leve coro vuelca
Qué voz de fuera del papel
nos contará tu fabricada infancia.
De qué ceñida proporción,
poliedro, eres ejemplo
o te escapas.

(Hagámosle creer que es parte del diseño,
que ha establecido conexión con los demás:
hagámosle creer que está vivo).

*Optimus artifex fecit** *[Escrito por el artista más grandioso.]

Poliedro

LOS SENTIDOS CORPORALES (5)

Nariz
¿cómo resuelves tus contradicciones?
Cerradura del aire,
¿cuál agujero es
camino de vida hacia arriba?
¿Cuál otro
por donde la muerte baja?
Falsa manera de entenderte.
Vida y muerte, juntas,
en tu interior suben y bajan.

Poliedro

MALA MEMORIA Y MALOS ACTORES

Repleto el ómnibus de gentes de todas las tribus
hermanadas en silenciosa soledad
adormecida la usual belicosidad por el cansancio

violentamente fueron abiertas las puertas
fuerte viento del sur
remolinos de arena lastimando los ojos
luces relampagueantes como letreros de neón
y una distorsionada voz
clamó potente a nuestras espaldas:

Which wise hypothesis, which geometry
will limit your duration and your space?
What music conductor will turn
your numbers into an ethereal chorus?
What voice outside of paper
will reveal to us your fabricated infancy?
From which close-fitting proportion,
polyhedron, are you an example,
or do you escape?

(Let's make it believe that it's part of the design,
that it has established a connection with the rest:
let's make it believe that it's alive).

Optimus artifex fecit [*Authored by the greatest artist*]

Poliedro

THE BODILY SENSES (5)

Nose
how to you resolve your contradictions?
Air lock,
which passage is
the road upward to life?
Through which other
does death descend?
It's a false way of understanding you.
Life and death, together
in your interior, go up and down.

Poliedro

BAD MEMORY AND BAD ACTORS

The bus is full of people from all tribes
matched exactly in silent loneliness
the usual bellicosity made sleepy by fatigue

violently the doors were opened
a strong south wind
whirlwinds of sand burning our eyes
flickering lights like neon signs
and a distorted voice
cried out loudly behind us:

otra vez el ilustre *stile antico*,
un barroco un tanto ingenuo
adaptado al uso local,
la divina exhuberancia con presupuesto recortado,
dos o tres estropeados ángeles
a punto de perder el equilibrio en la estribera

de modo que mi vecino de asiento y yo
nos miramos:

¿Es para usted el mensaje?
¿Es usted el profeta de turno?
¿Le toca a usted, o a mí?
Acaso seré yo, maestro?

Sofocos, codazos, empujones,
prodigios variados y signos de la época,
decisiones que tomar rápidamente
y nadie recuerda exactamente su papel.

Los ángeles resbalaron,
yacen aplastados en un cruce de calles,
un olor a plumas quemadas
e incienso sintético
insiste en no abandonar el aire adentro,
puertas chirriantes se abren y se cierran
y somos completamente diferentes
según el lado.

Poliedro

VARIACIÓN DEL MANDADERO GLOTÓN

te comiste los confites
apenas saliste de la casa

la crema blanca te parecía
gozosamente interminable
después que una señora
de azul y lavanda
te preguntaba tu nombre
(te pareció que preguntaba
mucho más que tu nombre)
ácido dardo, delicioso
en medio de dulzura insoportable,
la crema de dulzura insoportable,

again the illustrious *ancient style,*
baroque, just a bit naïve,
adapted to the local custom,
the divine exuberance with a budget cut,
two or three injured angels
about to lose their balance on the stirrups

so, the guy on the seat next to me and I
looked at each other:

Is the message for you?
Is it your turn to be the prophet?
Is it your turn or mine?
Can I be the one, my friend?

Suffocation, throwing of elbows, pushing
different signs and prodigies of the times,
decisions to be made quickly
and no one quite remembers his role.

The angels slipped,
they lie crushed on street intersections,
a smell of burnt feathers
and synthetic incense
insists on not leaving the air inside,
squeaky doors open and close
and we are completely different
according to which side we're on.

Poliedro

VARIATION OF THE GLUTTONOUS GO-FOR

you finished off the pastries
no sooner than you left the house.

the white cream seemed
joyfully unending
to you after a lady
in blue and lavendar
asked you your name;
(you thought she was asking about
much more than just your name)
a tart dart, so delicious
among such unbearable sweetness,
the cream of unbearable sweetness,

la crema de limón te atragantaba
cuando esperabas cruzar la avenida
sumergido en río caliente de gentes,
ruidos, señales difíciles de intepretar,
susurros de la otra esquina peligrosa—

el bizcochuelo esponjoso,
engañosamente sencillo,
plenamente fue saboreado y así conocido
con un poco de culpa
atravesando el parque sombrío
(rozando ansioso a enamorados,
tenías miedo de entenderlo
todo de pronto)

tragabas el relleno de chocolate y nueces
—un arte de cifrar toda música
en dos notas tan sólo—
cuando ya te habíamos visto en la esquina,
preparábamos la mesa, discursos,
un lugarcito entre nosotros y otros muertos,
y nuestra justa indignación en secreto:

porque no debías comerte la torta—
o al menos así de repente. . .
total,
era toda para vos,
desde el principio tuya:
pero de a poco, nene,
de a poco.

Música ficta

metahistorieta hiperculta post(u)moderna semicomics megakitsch polidramática politraumática paraliteraria transretorizante intertextual antiparnasiana hipertrófica antipirética epigástrica protonocutnra versificada profusamente anotada cuasi encantamiento y ensalmo celebratorio medio kachiäi de los decires cultos y de nación, glosas floriculturales y musicales ortopedias de robusta poética bien temperada al uso de los antiguos maestros de capilla flamencos y borgoñones y grecoguaraníticos puesta en materia poiética según la celebrada y gloriosa tectónica de la Casa Torta y el literario Mbaipy [mezcla] Parnasiano regados por abundante Zeitgeist de la mejor cosecha, id est *Secunda Reconstructio*:

the lemon cream was difficult to swallow
while you were waiting to cross the avenue,
submerged in a hot river of people,
noises, indecipherable signs,
murmurs from the other dangerous corner.

the spongy sponge cake,
deceptively simple,
was fully savored, and thus acquainted
with a bit of guilt
crossing the shady park
(slipping anxiously past lovers,
you were afraid to understand it
all at once).

you gobbled down the one with chocolate and nut filling
—the art of condensing all music
into just two notes—
when we had already spotted you on the corner,
we were preparing the table, the speeches,
a place between us and other corpses,
and our secret, justified indignation:

because you shouldn't have eaten the cake
—or at least so quickly—
in short,
it was all for you,
just for you, from the very beginning.
but just little by little, my dear,
just little by little.

Música ficta

meta short story hypercult post(u)modern semicomic megakitsch polydramatic polytraumatic paraliterary transrhetoricizing intertextual anti-Parnassian hypertrophic anti-pyretic epigastric protonocturn profusely versified annotated quasi enchantment and celebratory witchcraft half kachiäi of the cultured and national sayings, floricultural and musical glosses, orthopedics of robust, well-tempered poetics according to the old masters of Flemish, Burgundian and Greco-Guaranian chapels rendered in poetic matter according to the celebrated and glorious tectonic of the Cake House and the literary Parnassian mixture irrigated by an abundant Zeitgeist of the Best year, id est *Secunda Reconstructio*:

para ser leída y comentada y gozada y pro(e)scrita con metafóricos binóculos o quevedos de espanto de Islandia, mineral aqueste de crucero reconocidamente romboidal y propiedades curiosamente disdiaclásticas o de DOBLE REFRACCIÓN, según estudios de Bartholinus y Huygens[1]

de acuerdo en todo a las normas vigentes y reglamentaaciones dictadas por el buen uso en materia de arte y licencias del desdecir y oficios subordinados según testimonio de pareceres consultados y concordancia obrante en folios

imprimatur / nihil obstat / exequatur

diez por ciento para el autor y
el resto a Nuestras Obras de
Beneficiencia, Instrucción
Popular y Compra de Votos

con agradable y graciosa codetta conclusiva y primoroso
moñito midcult,
allaité al final,
para que todos entiendan

El mensaje.

[1] Officina Marulensis, Antwerpen, 1789.

hurras a bizancio

to be read and commented and enjoyed and pro(in)scribed with metaphorical binoculares or *pince nez* of Iceland spar, this mineral of recognizable rhomboidal cleavage and of curiously disdiaclastic properties or of DOUBLE REFRACTION, according to studies by Bartholinus and Huygens [1].

in accordance with all of the norms in effect and regulations dictated for proper use regarding art and licences of contradiction and subordinated posts according to the testimony of consulted verdicts and the functioning concordance in folios

imprimatur / nihil obstat / exequatur

ten per cent for the author and
the rest for Our Works of
Beneficence, Mass Education
and Purchase of Votes

with pleasant and gracious conclusive codetta and
exquisite midcult bow
over there at the end
for all those who understand

The Message.

[1] Officina Marulensis, Antwerp, 1789.

hurras a bizancio

AMANDA PEDROZO

POSIBILIDAD

Pudiera salir esta noche
con un varón reflexivo
dulcemente curioso.

Comeríamos cualquier cosa
en algún sitio descartable
terminaríamos codo a codo
debido al mal vino
y a las buenas palabras.

Yo sentiría
algún temblor de pecho de recuerdo
cuando llegara el momento
de tomarnos las manos.

Me preguntaría
si es por el frío o por lo nuevo.
yo tendría que cerrarme
la lengua
que no se me cayera al suelo
tu nombre.

Por eso
y porque estoy supercansada
de tanto repetir los mismos ritos
en idéntico orden
digo que no
que mañana hay mucho que hacer
y que me duermo me duermo.

Las cosas usuales

DUBITANDO

De mi muerte
que está siéndose desde siempre
me pregunto solamente
si habrá en el velatorio
alguna secreta repartición de panes
que estuve amasándole a la vida
con dudoso deleite.

Las cosas usuales

POSSIBILITY

I could go out tonight
with a reflective guy
sweetly curious.

We would eat anything at all
in some completely forgettable place
we would end up with our elbows together
due to the bad wine
and good conversation.

I would feel
a tremor in my breast as a souvenir
when the moment arrived
to hold hands.

I'd wonder if it were
because of the cold or the novelty.
I'd have to bite
my tongue
so your name wouldn't fall out
and hit the floor.

That's why
and because I'm super tired
of repeating the same rites
in identical order
I say no
'cause tomorrow there's a lot to do
and I'm going to sleep, I'm going to sleep.

Las cosas usuales

DOUBTING

About my death
that has been taking place forever
I only wonder
if during the wake there will be
some secret distribution of the bread
that I was kneading for life
with dubious delight.

Las cosas usuales

AD ETERNUM

A mi tío se le fueron
los ángeles al infierno
se muere de nostalgia anticipada
—es que tenía la esperanza
de aprender a tocar arpa
en el cielo—.

Dice que bebe de tristeza
pero se nota que anda triste
porque bebe.

Que el hombre es un pobre animal
que consigue soñarse a sí mismo
pero que es sueño sobre todo.

A mi tío le crecen pecados
como le crecen genuflexiones
le salen alas cuando apenas
está llegando a otro sitio
se duerme mirando las estrellas
y se pasa la vida negándose el ombligo.

Dice que tiene mala suerte
empyenamiento en las costillas
que no hay mujer que lo aguante
ni dinero que dure en sus bolsillos.

A mi tío se le cayeron
los ángeles al infierno
se muere de sudor anticipado
de consuelo de tontos
y dice que después de todo
sería superaburrido ponerse a tocar
el arpa
por los siglos de los siglos
amén.

Las cosas usuales

DESUBICACION

Aquí se estila
lavarse las axilas
por tiempo indefinido

AD ETERNUM

My uncle's angels
abandoned him and went straight to hell
he's dying of anticipated nostalgia
—it's just that he was hopeful
of learning to play the harp
in heaven.

He says that he drinks because he's sad
but it's clear that he's sad
because he drinks.

That man is a miserable animal
who succeeds at dreaming himself up
but who above all is a dream.

Sins grow on my uncle
just like genuflections do
wings sprout on him just when
he's arriving somewhere else
he goes to sleep looking at the stars
and he whiles away his life denying his belly button.

He says he has bad luck
empyema in his ribs
that no woman can put up with him
nor can money stay in his pockets.

My uncle's angels
fell upon him in hell
he's dying of anticipated sweat
of the consolation of fools
and he says that when all is said and done
it would be really boring to sit about playing
the harp
till the end of time
amen.

Las cosas usuales

OUT OF PLACE

Here it's customary
to wash your armpits
for an indefinite time

mientras se viva
y se acostumbra
el amor por cuotas
el vestido decorosamente
limpio
sin señales de pasto
ni de mariposas
o sea que todo
viene a ser
cuestión de estilo
y de mandamientos
por lo cual entiendo
razono
que aquí no quepo yo
con mis desobediencias lógicas
con mis amores completos.

Las cosas usuales

MAL DE AMORES, XII

Quiero que vuelvas
a tender tu cuerpo moreno
a mi orilla
en silencio
sin tantas historias
que contar.

Mal de amores

MAL DE AMORES, V

Llegas a mi vida
como un aguacero próximo
te observo llegar y es algo
irreversible
llegas y dispongo
mi mantel azulado en la mesa
el vino de los sueños
la copa de hierbas
mi cuenco de miel silvestre
mientras te observo llegar
desmedidamente
dibujando aromas y contornos
que serán pasto de tristeza
en mi boca

while one is alive
and one is accustomed to
love on regular payments,
to clothes decorously
clean
without any signs of grass
nor of butterflies,
in other words, everything
boils down to being
a question of style
and of commandments
by which I understand
I reason
that I don't fit in here
with my logical disobedience
with my complete loves.

Las cosas usuales

UNLUCKY AT LOVE, XII

I want you to lay your
brown body down again
at my side
in silence
without telling me
so many stories.

Mal de amores

UNLUCKY AT LOVE, V

You come into my life
like an imminent downpour
I see you coming and it's somewhat
irreversible
you arrive and I arrange
my bluish tablecloth on the table
my wine of dreams
the wine glass of herbs
my bowl of wildflower honey
while I watch you arrive
excessively
drawing aromas and surroundings
that will be the fodder of sadness
in my mouth

cuando al final te vayas
delicada
irremediablemente
de mi vida.

Mal de amores

MAL DE AMORES, XI

Te doblas
sobre mi cuerpo
como un lirio nuevo
y te recibo como un río
que piedras lleva
qué gozosa me descalzo
para andar por tu casa
me desprendo me abro
te consiento te invado
y dejo tu cuerpo
tendido como un lirio
a mi costado.

Mal de amores

ANTICIPACIONES, II

Uno sueña cada mañana
con pretextos alados
para no ir a la oficina
explicar por ejemplo
voy a hacerle el amor
a la vecina
y no puedo ir señor no puedo
mis miembros están ocupados
el amor es una emergencia
está antes que las órdenes
los jefes los salarios
la competencia y el aguinaldo.

Uno sueña en la manera
de hacer valer los sueños
apenas desprendidos
de la cama y la inocencia
vemos que se va el vecino
y deja un beso en la boca
de la mujer que amamos

when you finally leave
delicately
irremediably
from my life.

Mal de amores

UNLUCKY AT LOVE, XI

You bend
over my body
like a new iris
and I receive you like a river
that carries stones
how joyfully I remove my shoes
to walk through your house
I release myself I open myself
I indulge you I invade you
and I leave your body
lying like an iris
at my side.

Mal de amores

ANTICIPATIONS, II

One dreams every morning
with winged pretexts
for not going to the office
to explain for example
that I'm going to make love
to my neighbor
and I can't go sir I can't
my limbs are occupied
love is an emergency
it comes before orders
bosses, salaries
competition and the Christmas bonus.

One dreams up the way
to make dreams reality
as soon as they detach themselves
from the bed and from innocence
we see the neighbor leaving
and he plants a kiss on the mouth
of the woman we love

esa mujer que es salvia
pan y vino a los sentidos.

Uno sueña cada mañana
con llamar al jefe y decirle
el amor es esta alevosía
póngase en mi piel señor
y acabará estremecido
mordiéndole el esqueleto
y el ombligo a la vecina
y quizás entonces
mientras corro a tomar café
para espantar los sueños
usted llame a la oficina
y diga por ejemplo
que está labrando un verso
a cuchillazos y celos
para esa mujer que es salvia
pan y vino a los sentidos.

Mal de amores

DILACIONES, II

Si lo que me propones
es un amor Internet punto com y
arroba punto com y barra
y sobre todo tanta distancia
o pretendes un amor teléfono
con facturas por pagar
y recargo en línea tipo último aviso
si quieres que me queme la mirada
buscando tu encendido i-mail
en la computadora
si en vez de recorrer tu cuerpo debo
sobar ratones, teclas
y estar contenta como si te hubiera
tocado al infinito.

Si lo que me propones
no es soñar contigo pan y cebolla
ni celebrar los ritos
o desnudarnos hasta lo indecible.
Y quieres que te quiera
levemente tipo light anorexia

that woman, the sage
bread and wine of the senses.

One dreams every morning
about calling the boss and telling him
love is this treachery
put yourself in my skin sir
and you will end up astounded
biting the skeleton
and the belly button of your neighbor
and perhaps then
while I run out to have a coffee
to scare off my dreams
you'll call the office
and say for example
that you are cultivating a verse
with knife slashes and jealousy
for that woman who is the sage
bread and wine of the senses.

Mal de amores

DELAYS, II

If what you're proposing to me
is an Internet love dot com and
@ dot com and slash
and especially such a long distance
or you want a telephone love
with bills to pay
and on-line surcharges for last warnings
if you want me to burn my eyes out
searching for your inflamed e-mail
on the computer
if instead of traversing your body I have to
paw a mouse, a keyboard
and to be content as if I had touched
you ad infinitum.

If what you're proposing to me
is not to dream about you like our daily bread
nor to carry out the rites
nor to get nude together for the unmentionable.
And you want me to love you
ethereally, like light anorexia

entonces yo me voy
con mi cuerpo latino y mis excesos
y dejo que me extrañes
mientras buscas mi password
para decirme te amo
desde adentro
o meterme la lengua en el ombligo
arroba punto com
y así sabes que me voy a lo antiguo
con lágrimas y versos.

Mal de amores

then I'm leaving
with my Latin body and my excesses
and I'll let you miss me
while you're looking for my password
to tell me "I love you"
from within
or to place your tongue in my belly button
@ dot com
and that way you'll know that I'm leaving
the old-fashioned way,
with tears and verses.

Mal de amores

JACOBO RAUSKIN

LA NIÑA DE LOS MANGOS

a Osvaldo González Real

Hoy las hojas no son sino la imagen,
perdón, sonora
de la siesta y de un cántaro
a orillas de una sombra.
Caen,
caen los mangos
y se acerca una niña cuyo nombre ya no ignora
el ángel de su andar. Mira.
Ve los mangos.
Desnuda,
con sueño, confusa y aturdida
va por ellos.
Gira.
Gira y en sí misma se demora
si, cayendo,
entre frutas y a la siesta se abandona.
Lo sé.
¿Lo sabía?
Lo recuerdo
a orillas de una sombra
y en la siesta de los mangos.
La infancia duerme como fruta
y como árbol tiembla, despertando.

Naufragios

DE LA VIDA EN UN BOSQUE

Donde comienza el cuello y en la fina
columna del espasmo y de su fuego,
y donde muere sin su prisa un ruego
que por la lengua entonces no camina,

gozando cada glándula divina
goza la ninfa, sin ayer, sin luego.
Y el sátiro la sirve desde un ego
vuelto carne ¿Su suerte no adivina?

La ninfa, huye, desatando el crudo

THE GIRL WITH THE MANGOS

For Oswaldo González Real

Today the leaves are nothing but the image,
pardon me, the sound,
of the siesta and of the water pitcher
on the shores of a shadow.
The mangos fall,
                they fall,
and a girl—whose name her guardian
angel is not unaware of—approaches. She looks.
She sees the mangos.
                    Naked,
sleepy, confused and bewildered
she goes after them.
                    She spins.
She spins and within herself she tarries
falling,
among the fruit she surrenders to a siesta.
I know.
                Did I know it?
I remember
on the shores of a shadow
and in the siesta of the mangos.
Infancy sleeps like fruit
and like a tree, it trembles, awakening.

Naufragios

OF LIFE IN A FOREST

Where the neck begins and in the thin
column of the spasm and its fire,
and where a plea dies without any haste
and therefore can't pass over the tongue,

enjoying every divine gland,
he takes the nymph, with no yesterdays nor tomorrows.
And the satyr serves her, his ego
turns into flesh. Doesn't he know his fate?

The nymph flees, untying the crude

ego de un sátiro salido del llanto
que vuelve yermo cuanto fuera verde
y hastío cuanto fuese fuego. Rudo
y olvidado en un bosque, sin un canto,
por un amor que amando no se pierde.

Naufragios

DIÁLOGO INTERIOR (SIN COPLA)

Entre el tedio
y el encuentro,
uno ya miente diciendo:
no, no la quiero.

Y otro sopla
—en fiel silencio—
el muy oportuno
adverbio: *aún.*

Naufragios

LA INCREÍBLE VANIDAD DEL RITO HALLEY

Después de unos días, de un par de semanas,
un mes acaso, pierde el cometa
su atractiva caballera
y, calvo sideral, se aleja
para que tú puedas vivir con él
en una lámina.
Para que tu vida real se parezca
cada vez más a su fotografía.
Para oír cómo los niños recuerdan a sus padres
(si éstos lo vieron)
y aun a sus abuelos (si vieron,
dos veces, pasar por el cielo
el mismo cometa).

Jardín de la pereza

TORMENTA

No muy lejos del viento
abriendo la ventana,
tiemblan, hoy, dos naranjas

ego of a satyr, driven off by a cry
that turned everything green into wasteland
and into revulsion all that was fire. Rude
and forgotten in a forest, without a song,
for a love that, while still loving, will not be lost.

Naugragios

I NTERIOR DIALOGUE (WITHOUT VERSE)

Between tedium
and the encounter,
you lie when you say:
no, I don't love her.

And another whispers
—in faithful silence—
the very opportune
adverb: *yet.*

Naufragios

THE INCREDIBLE VANITY OF THE HALLEY RITE

After a few days, a few weeks,
perhaps a month, the comet loses
its attractive mane
and the sidereal baldy goes away,
so you can live with it
through an illustration.
So that your real life seems
more and more like its photo.
In order to hear how kids remember their parents
(if they saw it)
and even their grandparents (if they saw the
same comet pass twice
through the sky).

Jardín de la pereza

STORM

Not very far from the wind
opening the window today,
two oranges and a tablecloth

y un mantel: el invierno.
O sus flores, abiertas
en un cesto de mimbre,
entre hilos o venas
de otro azul desteñible.

Jardín de la pereza

JARDÍN DE LA PEREZA

Miro pasar el río
y una nube,
ciertas aves,

un bote,
algún camalote,

las victorias

regias e insufribles
entre las flores de la siesta
y el fardo de una tarde
sentimental y algodonera,

ex,

ex joven poeta,
ahora bardo estibador
de mi propia pereza,

y aprendo,
sí,

aprendo a descansar apenas,
a descansar hablando,
mintiendo,

dando tiempo al tiempo
entre una y otra changa de verdad.

¡Hay tan pocas
ahora!

Jardín de la pereza

tremble: winter.
Or winter's flowers, opened
in a wicker basket,
among threads or veins
of another fading blue.

Jardín de la pereza

THE GARDEN OF IDLENESS

I watch the river pass by
and a cloud,
some birds,

a rowboat,
a water hyacinth,

the Victoria Regia lilies

marvelous and unbearable
among the flowers of the siesta
and the bale of an afternoon,
sentimental and cottony,

ex,

ex young poet,
now a longshoreman bard
of my own idleness,

and I learn,
yes,

I hardly learn to rest,
to rest by speaking,
lying,

giving time to time itself
between this and that real jobs.

There are so few
now!

Jardín de la pereza

EL CELOSO

Loco de atar, pobre de amar, tonto de atarse y desatarse a su propia sombra y al divino botón, no calla las sospechas ridículas, da voz a las exclamaciones increíbles, se proyecta en las interjecciones del cretino social.
— Es un caso típico, dijo el psicólogo.
— Es un caso, redujo Psique.
— Es, dijo un tercero en concordancia.
Y el tiempo lo redujo al silencio conyugal, lo divorció.

La noche del viaje

LA RETICENCIA DE EROS

Se encontraron al pie de un árbol gigante. Ella partía, gajo a gajo, una mandarina; la iba chupando en paz, tal vez oía el murmullo de las hojas o el murmullo del río; él era incapaz de oír la diferencia, oía el viento. Le atraía el olor de la mujer, le disgustaba sin embargo el olor de la mandarina mezclado con el olor humano. Arrojó ella a las aguas la fruta a medio chupar y el río hizo un ruido como el de un caballo con el freno puesto. La hierba era fresca y el viento era cálido; el agua del río ofrecía dos temperaturas: una para ellos y otra para los peces. Y ellos no hablaron mucho; se bañaron antes y también después; caía el sol cuando se despidieron.

Tres idilios

CARTA

Él miente, ella dice la verdad, aquel otro escribe su poema de amor y lo quema, yo vivo mi amor y escribo una carta sobre la lluvia. Cuando se va la lluvia, escribo sobre el agua llovediza de los charcos. En habiendo el sol secado todo charco, escribo sobre el agua en otra parte; el agua mansa en los ojos de un caballo, el agua mínima de los arroyos de viñeta. Debo ser seguramente un corresponsal de viñeta, un enamorado de arroyo, un individuo pluvial.

La canción andariega

THE JEALOUS ONE

A raving lunatic, an unlucky lover, a poor soul who ties and unties himself to his own shadow and to nonsense, he doesn't keep his ridiculous suspicions quiet, he voices his incredible exclamations, pushes his way in with interjections of a social cretin.
"He's a typical case," said the shrink
"He's a case," synthesized Psyche
"He is," said a third in agreement.
And time reduced him to conjugal silence; she divorced him.

La noche del viaje

THE RETICENCE OF EROS

They met at the foot of a gigantic tree. She was opening, section by section, a tangerine; munching on it calmly, perhaps she heard the murmur of the leaves or of the river; he was incapable of hearing the difference, he heard the wind. The scent of the woman attracted him, however, the scent of the tangerine blended with the human smell disgusted him. She threw the half-chewed fruit into the water and the river replied like a horse with its bit in place. The grass was fresh, the wind warm; the river offered two temperatures: one for them, the other for the fish. And they didn't speak much; they bathed before, and also afterwards; the sun was setting when they said goodbye.

Tres idilios

LETTER

He lies, she tells the truth, the other guy writes his love poem and he burns it, I live my love and I write a letter about the rain. When the rain departs, I write about the puddles of rain water. Once the sun has dried all the puddles, I write about the water in some other place; the gentle water in the eyes of a horse, the minimal water of the streams of a vignette. I must surely be a correspondent of vignettes, a lover of streams, a pluvial individual.

La canción andariega

CANCIÓN

Se fue, se ha ido la lluvia. En mínimos huertos, en patios ínfimos, en jardines francamente empantanables y en aceras usurpadas por baldíos, el gorrión la recuerda.

Δ Δ Δ

MAÑANITA

La vieja lleva un haz de leña sobre la cabeza y tiene un cigarro sin encender entre los labios. Cambió el arte, pienso, pues ya no la representa, pero no cambió ella. Y sigue su camino: va por la parte baja de la cañada, a ratos moja el pie en el agua del arroyo.

Alegría de un hombre que vuelve

PRELUDIO

Cuando llegaron a *La isla* (el nombre le viene bien a tal supermercado), qué sino temor en el pecho y tufo de cebollas podridas en un rincón. De todos modos, habrán gritado ¡Manos arriba! El más joven golpeó a la cajera y se llevó el dinero mientras el socio, idiotizado por el gatillo, disparaba al aire. Años después, la identidad de los asaltantes seguía siendo un enigma; ni siquiera se pudo hacer el identikit: los testigos no recordaban los rostros. El caso fue al olvido, con razón. Si ahora lo menciono, es porque mi memoria no es tan mala y porque quiero hablar de la violencia y del olvido como preludio de un encantamiento. No supone otra cosa salir hoy de ese supermercado y ver a la luna en la ciudad de los grillos, de los baldíos, en la simple callejería de una emoción, en las horas de una bella esperanza.

Δ Δ Δ

AYER

Los baldíos, aquellos grandes
y abolidos baldíos de mi infancia,
nada, ya nada son sino este canto,
este abuso de la nostalgia.

Salvar quisiera su memoria
y más que su memoria su penumbra

SONG

It left, the rain has left. In miniscule orchards, in tiny patios, in gardens frankly swampable, and on sidewalks, overtaken by vacant lots, the sparrow remembers it.

Δ Δ Δ

THE WEE SMALL HOURS

The old woman carries a bundle of firewood upon her head, an unlit cigarette between her lips. Art has changed, I reflect, because it no longer portrays her, but she hasn't changed. And she goes on her way: down to the deepest part of the ravine, stopping a while to wet her foot in the stream.

Alegría de un hombre que vuelve

PRELUDE

When they arrived at *La isla* (the name fits well for such a supermarket), what was there if not fear in one's breast and the stench of rotting onions in a corner? Anyhow, they probably shouted: "Hands up!" The youngest one hit the cashier and took the money while his partner, stupefied by the trigger, kept shooting in the air. Years later, the identity of the robbers remained an enigma; they weren't even able to make an identity profile: the witnesses didn't remember their faces. Of course, the case was forgotten. If I mention it now, it's because my memory is not so bad and I want to discuss violence and forgetfulness as a prelude to enchantment. It implies nothing other than to leave that supermarket today and to see the moon in this city of crickets, of empty lots, in the simple wandering around the streets of an emotion, in the hours of a beautiful hope.

Δ Δ Δ

YESTERDAY

The vacant lots, those big
and abolished vacant lots of my infancy,
nothing, they are no longer anything but this song,
this abuse of nostalgia.

I'd like to save their memory
and more than their memory, their penumbra

con la de un patio y un jardín
bajo la luna.

En el ayer de los baldíos
canto un hogar que nunca fue
y fue también el mío.

Eran baldíos limpios, dignos.
Incluso con algún hereditario
decoro hipotecario.

Fogata y dormidero de caminantes

LECHO Y LITERATURA

C'est un livre qu'au lit on lit
Apollinaire

El futuro durmiente, si es sincero,
dormita o lee un rato, luego duerme
como si entrara en el último sueño.
Es grato y oportuno leer así en la cama.
No, no depende tanto del libro,
cuenta más una buena almohada,
poesía hay siempre en las estrellas
que caben en un tomo de bolsillo
o en un formato de ventana.
Leer, leer con gusto en la divina
presencia compañera que nos dice:
"Léeme ahora el cuerpo, bien, sin prisa."

La calle del violín allá lejos

BELLEZA DE AYER

La puerta de calle tenía la magia de su número. Y el árbol frente a la puerta, en los días de viento dulce, soltaba un recuerdo de las Hespérides. Casa grande, alta, quizá muy honda. Casa vieja, el techo era una viñeta de otros años, de otros años era el patio enjardinado con un rosal. La frecuentaba mi admiración, aunque siempre de paso y desde la acera. Desapareció en mil novecientos ochenta y seis, la mató la fiebre edilicia.

Δ Δ Δ

with that of a patio and a garden
under the moon.

In the yesterday of the vacant lots
I sing of a home that never was,
yet it was mine.

They were clean vacant lots, dignified.
Including a hereditary,
mortgage-laden decorum.

Fogata y dormidero de caminantes

BED AND LITERATURE

C'est un livre qu'au lit on lit
Apollinaire

The man who will soon be asleep, if he is sincere,
dozes or reads a little, then sleeps
as though he had entered the last sleep.
It's pleasant and opportune to read that way in bed.
No, it doesn't depend so much on the book,
it relies more on a good pillow,
there is always poetry in the stars
that fits in a pocketbook,
or in the format of a window.
To read, to read with pleasure in the divine
companion presence that tells us:
"Read my body now; well, without haste."

La calle del violín allá lejos

YESTERDAY'S BEAUTY

The street door had the magic of its address. And the tree in front of the door, in the days of sweet wind, released a memory of the Hesperides. A big house, tall, perhaps very deep. An old house, the roof was a vignette of another time; of another time was the patio, made into a garden by a rosebush. My admiration went there frequently, if only momentarily and from the sidewalk. It disappeared in nineteen eighty six, killed by a municipal fever.

Δ Δ Δ

ALFREDO* ENVEJECE

La efigie sustentada
por mil portaestandartes
pierde fuerza y color.

Los años atenúan
el rictus militante
y el gran perdonavidas
se muestra viejo al sol.

Δ Δ Δ

RIMAS TOTALITARIAS

El único partido
político admitido.

El de la gente muda
y servicial, oscura.

Recordada en metáforas,
melopeas o anáforas.

Δ Δ Δ

ADAGIO

Un día entre los muchos días grises,
volviendo de quién sabe dónde,
pasé por unas calles tristes, tristísimas.
Puertas que nadie abría,
ventanas contra un cielo abolido
y flores viejas a la vera de un bar.
Fue inútil ofrecerme entonces
a la musa del llanto.
Fue tan inútil que no pude
dar mi voz a una queja siquiera.
El amor, la pasión, la canción,
todo era de un violín invisible,
un violín allá lejos.
De mi sólo salían silencios.
De mí, con la esperanza de otros días.

La calle del violín allá lejos

*Alfredo Stroessner

ALFREDO AGES

The effigy sustained
by a thousand standard bearers
loses its force and color.

The years attenuate
the militant rictus
and the great bully
looks old in the sun.

Δ Δ Δ

TOTALITARIAN RHYMES

The only political
party permitted.

The one of muted people,
willing to serve, obscure.

Remembered in metaphors,
monotonous singing or in anaphoras

Δ Δ Δ

ADAGIO

One day among many gray days,
returning from who knows where,
I passed through some sad streets, very sad.
The doors that nobody opened,
windows facing an abolished sky,
and old flowers along the wall of a bar.
It was useless then to offer myself
to the muse of weeping.
It was so useless I couldn't
even voice a complaint.
Love, passion, song,
everything was from an invisible violin,
a violin far away.
From me only silences came out.
From me, with the hope of another day.

La calle del violín allá lejos

*Alfredo Stroessner

VERDE PRADERA INTERMINABLE

La quieren los labriegos sin tierra.
La regatea un gran terrateniente.
La ficha un hi.. de pu.. en un ministerio.
La sobrevuela un cuervo.
Mirándola, recuerdo estas palabras
y al tirano que ayer las decía:
"La tierra es buena, el hombre es bueno."

Adiós a la cigarra

Δ Δ Δ

LA PLAZA

a Susana Gertopan

La tarde te conoce mejor que yo.
Me conoce mejor que tú,
y nos junta, ya somos miles,
millones en el mundo.
Mundo instantáneo que nos da una identidad momentánea;
somos la gente de la plaza en la tarde del mundo.
La plaza, con sus cuatro calles como cuatro paredes,
termina siendo el patio de la ciudad.
Y el niño que llora intajablemente
Y el anciano que sonríe para no pensar.
Es la estatua que nunca dice nada.
Es la pareja que aún se ama.
Es el viento, amable a ratos.
Arriba el cielo, abajo un árbol.
Y la tarde, diciéndonos que no se va.
O que no quiere irse, que no es lo mismo.

Pitogüé

THE GREEN, INTERMINABLE PRARIE

The landless farm workers want it.
A great land owner bargains for it.
A son of a b. . . in a ministry archives it.
A crow flies over it.
Looking at it, I remember these words
and the tyrant who back then pronounced them:
"The land is good, man is good."

Adiós a la cigarra

Δ Δ Δ

THE TOWN SQUARE

for Susana Gertopan

The afternoon knows you better than I do.
It knows me better than you do,
and it gathers us, we are thousands,
millions in the world.
An instantaneous world that gives us a momentary identity;
we're the town square people in the afternoon of the world.
The town square, with its four streets like four walls,
ends up being the patio of the town.
And the kid who ceaselessly cries.
And the old man who smiles to avoid thinking.
It's the statue that never says anything.
It's the couple that's still in love.
It's the wind, at times friendly.
The sky above, a tree below.
And the afternoon, telling us it won't go away.
Or that it doesn't want to, which is not the same thing.

Pitogüé

JUNTOS

Algo le dice el viento a la lluvia
y no sabemos qué, no sabemos mucho más
del hombre y la mujer que ahí cruzan la calle
bajo un solo paraguas.
Se aman, sólo quieren estar juntos.
Y se parecen a la lluvia:
son interminablemente momentáneos.

Doña Ilusión

TOGETHER

The wind says something to the rain
and we don't know what, we don't know much more
about the man and the woman who cross the street over here
under a single umbrella.
They love each other, they only want to be together.
And they resemble the rain:
they are interminably momentary.

Doña Ilusión

ELVIO ROMERO

YA EN EL CAMINO. . .II

Solo el paraguayo.
Con un par de guitarras sobre el hombro
—sacudiéndose el polvo de todos los desvelos—
camina oliendo a tierra,
a selva todavía;
en una pulsará su tristeza profunda,
en otra, su rebeldía antigua como su tierra.

Una imagen de cruces y medallas
caída del follaje forestal
transpone los umbrales de sus pupilas hondas,
le fija una atadura,
le rubrica una amarra de recuerdos amargos.

Autorizado por la voz que sale
de grietas dibujadas sobre muros quebrados
—tatuado a golpe de hachas,
con la antigua sonrisa demolida,
con el pecho marcado por demolida herrumbre—,
llega con una voz de entraña apretujada
y con una canción de llamarada errante.

Es como si saliera de un barranco,
de patios deshabitados y sin ecos perpetuos;
resucitado de un relámpago,
de un gajo desprendido
como un rayo de luz de una órbita vacía.

Nada sobre su frente que no hable de dureza.
Nada que nos recuerde cuanto no sea denso.
Nada en su mano dura que no hable de sudores.
Nada que lleve a olvido su condición de errante.

Todo él, metal cortante; filo final, seguro:
funda de empuñadura.

Días roturados

****

ON THE ROAD NOW. . . II

And the Paraguayan alone.
With a pair of guitars on his back
—brushing off the dust from all his sleeplessness—
he walks still smelling of earth,
of jungle;
on one he'll strum his profound sadness,
on the other, his old rebellion, like his land.

An image of crosses and medallions
fallen from the forest's foliage
transposes the thresholds of his deep pupils,
a cord fastens him,
a rope encircles him with bitter memories.

Authorized by a voice that comes out
of cracks drawn upon the broken walls
—tattooed with hatchet blows,
with his old demolished smile,
with his chest marked by demolished rust—
he arrives with a voice of squeezed viscera
and with a song of an errant flame.

It's as though he came out of a gorge,
of uninhabited patios and without perpetual echoes;
resuscitated from a lightening bolt,
from a fallen branch,
like a ray of light from an empty orbit.

Nothing on his forehead belies his grit.
Nothing to remind us of things not solid.
Nothing in his hard hand not suggestive of sweat.
Nothing to be forgotten of his errant ways.

All of him, cutting metal; final edge, sure:
sheath of a weapon.

Días roturados

****

CANTO EN EL SUR

Esta noche, en el Sur,
me he mirado en tus ojos.

Soy como tú,
de piel morena, oscura, oscura,
con estrellas heridas por adentro
y por fuera sudor, cáscara ruda.

Tengo la sangre hirviendo
como un sinuoso trueno derramado;
tengo las manos ásperas
como herramientas duras y soleadas;
tengo los ojos lúbricos
como lúbricas raíces.

Esta noche, en el Sur,
me he mirado en tus ojos.

Te vi ayer en el Norte;
vi en el Norte lo mismo, el mismo
y primario dolor sobre los cuerpos,
el aguardiente galopando a sorbos
y lo demás lo mismo: el mismo
brazo sudando a contraluz sangrienta,
el mayoral que brama entre los árboles,
los mismos ojos sin calor, la misma
temblorosa epilepsia del sudor,
los mismos exprimidos, los mismos coronados!

Esta noche, en el sur,
me he mirado en tus ojos.

Soy como tú,
la misma turbulencia contra el mismo espejismo,
idéntico remanso bajo la misma noche.

Conservo el sortilegio
de estas zonas arbóreas que me cercan.
Tengo la risa ronca
y estas anchas tristezas.
De piel morena, oscura,
pisando en el calor exasperado.

Resoles Áridos

A SONG DOWN SOUTH

Tonight, down South,
I've looked at myself in your eyes.

I am like you,
dark skin, dark, dark,
with wounded stars inside
and on the outside, sweat, a rough rind.

My blood is boiling
like a sinuous, scattered thunderbolt;
my hands are rough,
hard as sun-basked tools;
my eyes lubricious
like lubricious roots.

Tonight, in the South,
I've looked at myself in your eyes.

I saw you yesterday in the North;
I saw the same thing in the North, the same
primary pain on the bodies,
the cane alcohol galloping by sips
and all the rest the same: the same
arm sweating, bloody under the light,
the foreman who roars among the trees,
the same eyes without warmth, the same
jittery epilepsy of sweat,
the same people oppressed, the same ones crowned!

Tonight, in the South,
I've looked at myself in your eyes.

I am like you,
the same turbulence against the same mirage,
the identical calm under the same night.

I conserve the sorcery
of these arboreal zones that surround me.
I have a hoarse laughter
and broad sorrows.
Of dark skin, dark,
stepping into the exasperated warmth.

Resoles Áridos

CUANDO ESTÁS LEJOS

Aquella extraña, extraña callejuela
que conocimos en país lejano,
tenía un faro en un portal derruido
como un recuerdo marinero y vano
de alguna luz que extravió su estela
yendo a parar en muro destruido.

Vuelvo a esta callejuela triste, triste
(¡qué no diera por ver su sombra pura!)
hoy que preciso de una lumbre plena,
de aquella tuya, aquella que me diste
cuando la tarde se me puso oscura
con no sé qué color de pobre arena.

Vuelvo a esa callejuela ahora, ahora
(resto de sombras que otro tiempo viera)
como buscando aquella luz perdida
por la que diera todo en esta hora
alrededor de mí, por la que diera
—con no sé qué color— sombra y herida. . .

Un relámpago herido

ALLÁ

DEBE, allá, estar lloviendo;
sin pausa estar lloviendo, lloviznando
en los bosques,
sobre las casas pobres, abotonándose
la noche y mesándose la barba envejecida
en los obrajes, allá lejos, lloviendo,
lloviznando en la noche.

Y habrá ya anochecido.
Siempre se me ha hecho tarde entre los tilos
serranos, a la hora de volver, anochecido,
allá lejos, cuando aún no sabía
que no fuera a volver, que se ha hecho tarde
lloviendo, anocheciendo.

En la noche, allá lejos, lloviznando.

Destierro y atardecer

WHEN YOU ARE FAR AWAY

THAT strange, strange little street
that we found in a distant country,
had a lamp in a doorway in ruins
like a memory, seaworthy and vain,
of some light that misplaced its wake
on its way to pose on a crumbled wall.

I return to that little street, so sad, sad
(what I wouldn't give to see its pure shadow!)
today when I need a bright light,
of that one of yours, that one you gave me
when the afternoon darkened on me
with who knows what color of poor sand.

I return to that little street, now, now
(a remainder of shadows I had seen once before)
as though looking for that lost light,
for which, right now, I'd surrender everything
around me, for which I'd give
—who knows what color—a shadow, a wound.

Un relámpago herido

OVER THERE

Over there, it should be raining;
raining without pause, drizzling
in the forests,
upon the poor houses, the night buttoning up,
tugging on its aged beard,
upon the lumber camps, far away, raining,
drizzling through the night.

And already it's probably night.
Night always caught me under the mountain lindens,
at the time for returning, nightfall, far away,
when I was still unaware that I wouldn't return,
that it was late,
raining, getting dark.

At night, far away, drizzling.

Destierro y atardecer

REQUIEM PARA UN TITIRITERO

En la casa de la colina
desde ayer habita la muerte,
el viento
desgasta un telón verde;
hay un tinglado triste,
vacío, que se mece,
en la casa de la colina
donde una flor morada crece.

En la casa de la colina
hay rincones que palidecen,
un halo
de luna el techo envuelve,
hay Príncipes y Reinas
y Arlequines con fiebre,
en la casa de la colina
por donde el tiempo se detiene.

En la casa de la colina
sube el musgo por las paredes,
la noche
penetra y se conmueve;
hay fantoches que saca
el guante a la intemperie,
en la casa de la colina
donde un retablo se oscurece.

En la casa de la colina
la desdicha tejió sus redes,
el aire
se detiene y se hiere;
hay un hondo silencio
de pantomima inerte
en la casa de la colina
donde la sombra se estremece.

En la casa de la colina
corre el frío por los dinteles,
la luz
da un traspié y retrocede;
hay un traje vacío,
un Corcel sin jinete,
¡en la casa de la colina
que da vuelta y desaparece!

REQUIEM FOR A PUPPETEER

In the house on the hill
since yesterday death has dwelled,
the wind
ravages a green drop-curtain;
there's a sad stage,
empty, it rocks to and fro,
in the house on the hill
where a purple flower grows.

In the house on the hill
where nooks grow pale,
a halo
from the moon envelops the roof,
there are Princes and Queens
and feverish Harlequins,
in the house on the hill
where time stands still.

In the house on the hill
moss creeps up the walls,
night
pierces and is sadly touched;
there are puppets that a glove
takes out in foul weather
from the house on the hill
where the stage darkens.

In the house on the hill
misfortune has cast its webs,
the air
comes to a halt and is wounded;
there reigns a deep silence
of inert pantomime,
in the house on the hill
where a shadow trembles.

In the house on the hill
cold creeps through the lintels,
light
stumbles and backs out;
there is an empty suit,
a steed with no rider,
in the house on the hill
that turns around and disappears!

DE UNA FLAUTA Y UN PÁJARO

De un terreno escondido
provenía el sonido de la flauta,
del guayabal, desde un poniente en llamas;
de aquella flauta y su estremecimiento
casi tangible y doloroso, del
aire herido que atravesó la calandria
en su vuelo de amor; de allá provino
el eco triste, el melancólico acento y el gemido
de la flauta del ciego, la melodía acongojada y honda
del hombre en el solar, del hombre anónimo en el
valle, y allí mismo, en la siesta,
encontramos al pájaro caído, en el ardiente verano
—latido de colores yaciente sobre el pasto—,
aún con el cuerpo tibio, agonizante;
al pájaro, al cautivo
también de aquella música silvestre, al pájaro
yaciente en la red de esa música, de ese doliente
acento, al pájaro caído en su vuelo de amor, atento
al eco triste, a aquel sonido largo
de flauta infausta y triste, pertinaz, desolada en el verano.

Los valles imaginarios

OF A FLUTE AND A BIRD

From a hidden land
came the sound of a flute,
from the guava grove, from a flaming sunset;
from that flute and its almost tangible
and painful quivering, from the
wounded air where the lark crossed through
on its flight of love; from over there returned
its sad echo, the melancholic accent and sigh
of the blind man's flute, the anguished, deep melody
of the man in his ancestral home, of the anonymous man
in the valley, and right there, in his siesta,
we find the fallen bird, in the burning summer
—a pulse of colors collapsed on the grass—
with its body still warm, in agony;
the bird, also a captive
of that untamed music, of that mournful
accent, the fallen bird in its flight of love, heeding
the sad echo, that long sound
of the accursed, sad flute, persistent, desolate in the summer.

Los valles imaginarios

RICARDO DE LA VEGA

II

Al caminar por la vereda y detenerme
a comprar cigarrillos o un periódico,
veo un ademán distinto, una actitud
dentro de mí, y ajena,
que ha cambiado.
Algo así como una forma de enfrentar
o de aceptar las situaciones tal cual son.
Algunos llaman a esto madurez; otros,
cobardía. Yo, sin saber qué nombre darle,
contemplo, con asombro,
a estas manos y sus rumbos casi independientes
al hurgar en el bolsillo
o al entregar unas monedas.
Mas,
para qué empeñarme
en dibujar correctos movimientos en el aire
si éstos, tal vez sean
el último eslabón
de una cadena
que comienza más allá
de mí.
        (Lo inasible
                        toma a veces la forma del amor.)
Ahora cruzo la calle. El viento
dejándose caer entre las hojas, marcha.

Sin opciones después de la cena

UN CHANTA

Cuando cierren los pubs y los casinos
y las boites sean hospitales o museos
¿qué he de hacer para pasarla bien?
¿Y si a los automóviles de los chantas se les prohibe
el estacionamiento?
¿Tendré que girar
girando hasta desaparecer?
¿Qué pasará cuando las escaleras
que me llevan al trabajo,
al bar
o al reservado, no tengan final?

II

When I walk down the sidewalk and stop
to buy cigarettes or a newspaper,
I see in myself a distinct look, an attitude
inside of me, and outside,
that has changed.
Something like a way of facing
or accepting situations just as they are.
Some would call this maturity; others,
cowardice. I, without knowing how to call it,
contemplate with surprise
these hands and their almost independent movements
when they dig around in my pockets
or when they hand over some coins.
But,
why should I insist
on drawing correct movements in the air
if they are perhaps
the last link
in a chain
that begins beyond
me.
(The ungraspable
sometimes takes the form of love.)
Now I cross the street. The wind
dropping in among the leaves, marches on.

Sin opciones después de la cena

A SHOWOFF

When they close the pubs and the casinos
and the nightclubs become hospitals or museums,
what am I supposed to do to have a good time?
And if they prohibit parking for the flashy cars?

Will I have to go round and round
until I disappear?
What's going to happen when the stairs
—the ones that lead me to work,
to the bar or
to that seedy hotel—turn out to be endless?

Preguntarme estas cosas es un chiste,
una broma.

Ahora todo está definido: mi hogar,
los amigos,
la marca de mis camisas, mis amantes;
ahora me vendo de a poco
sin importar casi si me señalan,
ahora el mundo me importa cada vez menos;
ahora
encenderé un cigarrillo y estiraré las piernas:
ceniceros de plata
y luces perfectas, sí,
pero a veces me canso,
y a nadie engaño con mi triste mirada
o cuando digo que me aburren
las historias de sumas,
restas, cuernos o divisiones.

¿Acaso pueda ser ineficaz
y negarme a cumplir alguna orden superior?
No, ahora ya no.
Además, ¿para qué?

Sin opciones después de la cena

UN TRAIDOR PIENSA

Puede que abras
o cierres alguna puerta.
Puede que tus pasos
dibujen prontamente huellas
en la noche.
Se hace tarde, te dices.
Desde una ventana te saluda tu hijo
él no puede imaginar nada.
En un zaguán se duerme un perro
y en los focos, mariposas ciegas, giran.
No, no hace frío.
Un cigarrillo juega en tu boca.
Casi te veo:
        acaso silbes.
Acaso rías al pensar que tu mujer
está celosa. "Estas no son horas
para ver a un amigo", te dijo al salir.
Acaso pienses que la noche

Wondering about these things is a joke,
a jest.

Now everything is defined: my home,
friends,
the brand name of my shirts, my lovers;
now I sell myself for very little
not really bothered if people point at me,
now everything matters less and less to me;
now
I'll light a cigarette and I'll stretch my legs:
silver ashtrays
and perfect lighting, yes,
but sometimes I tire,
and I don't fool anybody with my sad face
or when I say that stories of addition,
subtraction, cuckoldry, or division
bore me.

Can I possibly be inefficient
and refuse to comply with my boss's orders?
No, not any longer.
But then, why would I?

Sin opciones después de la cena

A TRAITOR THINKS

It's possible you open
or close some door.
It's possible your steps
promptly draw footprints
in the night.
It's getting late, you tell yourself.
From a window your son greets you;
he can't imagine anything.
In a doorway a dog falls asleep
and around the light bulbs blind butterflies circle.
No, it isn't cold.
A cigarette bounces around in your mouth.
I almost see you:
     maybe you're whistling.
Maybe you'll laugh when you think your wife
is jealous. "This is no time
to visit a friend," she said when you left.
Maybe you think the night

es sólo una excusa que me dicta el miedo.
Acaso tengas miedo...

Hay en el cielo una quietud extraña,
un silencio extraño.
Das vuelta una esquina,
cruzas la calle.
Ya no sabes la hora.
Ya no sabes qué pasará mañana.
No sabes que el silencio es una trampa,
que la libertad es una eterna trampa,
que los puñetazos pueden más que el amor,
pueden más que mis sueños.
Hermano, no sabes,
que tus pasos
miden el tiempo de los que te esperan,
de los que sabiamente tejen
mi piel golpe a golpe.
No sabes que han rodeado la cuadra,
no sabes
que a pesar de las cosas que compartimos juntos,
que a pesar de todo
que a pesar de todo
yo
te delato.

Sin opciones después de la cena

A UN POETA CONTESTATARIO

Tú estás ahí
enarbolando al viento
el pecho abierto y la mirada rebelde.
Casi de piedra y lágrimas.
Yo aquí
con mis corbatas viejas,
mis libros,
mi horario cotidiano,
mis cuentas...
Tú por las calles
por la aurora,
libre del televisor y la heladera.
Yo aquí
sin la certeza—ésa que tú posees—
de un mundo mejor.
Yo aquí
dudando—y en esto, oh terco hermano, no me igualas—,

is just an excuse that fear imposes on me.
Maybe you're afraid. . .

There is a strange peace in heaven,
a strange silence.
You turn a corner,
and cross the street.
You no longer know what time it is.
You no longer know what will happen tomorrow.
You don't know that silence is a trap,
that liberty is an eternal trap,
that beatings accomplish more than love,
more than my dreams.
Brother, you don't know,
that your steps
are marking time for those who wait for you,
for those who wisely weave
my flesh blow by blow.
You don't know they have surrounded the block,
you don't know
that in spite of the things we share,
that in spite of everything,
that in spite of everything,
I
will denounce you.

Sin opciones después de la cena

TO ONE WHO WRITES PROTEST POETRY

You are there
exposing to the wind
your naked chest and rebellious look.
Almost of stone and tears.
Here I am
with my old neckties,
my books,
my daily schedule,
my bills. . .
You, in the streets
at dawn,
free from the TV and the fridge.
Here I am
without any certainty—like that one you possess—
of a better world.
Here I am
doubting—and when I do, oh stubborn brother, you're not my equal—

preguntádome, ¿para qué sirven los poemas?

Yo desde aquí
te veo —nos vemos—
en soledad muriendo.

Sin opciones después de la cena

NOTABLE PARAÍSO (fragmento)

Todo está bien aquí,
si callas.

Es esta paz un ángel que se quema
un viento, un vaso, un árbol que se queman
y nosotros andando
hechos cenizas, humo,
caminando
entre manteles, alas,
vino que se evapora
al escuchar
que se repita la orden
de beber,
de beber y callar
hasta que duermas,
hasta que sueñes que se abren las puertas
de las calles
que nunca terminas de cruzar,
pues, pasa un colectivo,
o pasa un coche raudo y otro y otro
o te detiene el miedo
o acaso una palabra;
(a veces no terminan nunca de cruzar
las palabras...)

Nadie puede explicar cómo es que vamos
al trabajo;
cómo se encuentran allí nuestras pisadas,
cómo es que cambian nuestras huellas
en los baños y en cada picaporte.

Y en cada vidrio que anhelamos trizar,
mas, te devuelve, irremediable, el rostro
y te vuelve el miedo
y te vuelve el viento que empujará tus
pasos a

wondering what poems are for.

From here
I see you—we see each other—
dying in solitude.

Sin opciones después de la cena

NOTABLE PARADISE (fragment)

Everything's fine here,
if you're quiet.

This peace is a burning angel,
a wind, a glass and a tree that burn
and we go on
converted into ashes, smoke,
walking
among tablecloths, wings,
wine that evaporates
when we hear
that the order to drink
is repeated,
to drink and to shut up
until you fall asleep,
until you dream that the doors to the streets
are opened,
that you can never quite cross,
because a bus passes,
or a loud car passes and another and another
or fear stops you,
or perhaps a word;
(sometimes words never stop
crossing. . .)

No one can explain how it is that we go
to work;
how our footsteps are found there,
how it is our fingerprints change
in the bathrooms and on every doorknob.

And in every window that we long to shatter,
but it irremediably returns your face to you
and fear returns to you
and the wind that will push your
steps toward

la muerte
y te devuelve el rostro,
el vuelto, la propina del día.
Nadie puede explicar
por qué
nadie cruza estas calles.

Nadie quiere contarnos por qué y en dónde
se nos mueren esos ángeles tercos,
esos ángeles de la ribera
de los bares...

Esos atrevidos ángeles de la madrugada.

Es esta paz del ángel que nos quema,
que nos dibuja en llamas;
que nos envía traidores a la cama
y nos escupe
el beso mandón
en nuestros labios;
es esta paz del ángel que nos quema,
ése: el de los brazos como ríos,
pero al revés
porque recorre
tu cuerpo, tu casa, tu jardín
y te desprende el saco
y ya te lleva el libro preferido,
y te abre la camisa
y te besa
y te seca.
Es esta paz el beso permanente,
lentísimo, de fuego.

Notable paraíso

A UNAS CUADRAS DE PALMA Y COLÓN

Una manito limpia el parabrisas
con un apuro que le viene del cielo.
Limpia el barro y las hojas.
Raspa con las uñas
los restos de los pajaritos.
Los niños y los pajaritos
se entretienen, a veces,
demasiado sobre tu vida,

death
and it returns your face to you,
your loose change, the gratuity of the day.
No one can explain
why
no one crosses these streets.

No one wants to tell us why and where
those stubborn angels will die on us,
those angels from the shore
of the bars...

Those daring angels of dawn.

It's this angel's peace that burns us,
that draws our portrait with flames;
that sends traitors to our bed
and that spits
an imperious kiss
on our lips;
it's this angel's peace that burns us,
that one: the one with arms like rivers,
but backwards
because it runs through
your body, your house, your garden
and it takes off your jacket
and now it brings your favorite book,
and it opens your shirt
and kisses you
and dries you.
In this peace the permanent kiss,
very slow, of fire.

Notable paraíso

A FEW BLOCKS FROM PALMA AND COLON

A little hand cleans the windshield
with a haste descended from heaven.
It cleans the mud and the leaves.
With its fingernails, it scrapes
the residue of the little birds.
Kids and little birds
sometimes amuse themselves
too much at your expense,

y es así que alzas tu voz para espantarlos,
y van hacia la radio, los espejos,
pero ellos siguen allí con su tarea
las ruinas de tus suspiros
y el humo de tus poemas.
Hay días en que nada los detiene
y arremeten con sus alas
hasta limpiarnos de ti, de mí,
de todo lo que es sucio y sueña.

Afuera

LA FIESTA ES AFUERA

Golpea la piñata
con tus pequeñas dudas:
como de una flor saldrán las beneméritas
palabras que anuncien el Verbo;
de su barriga, el talco, irrumpirá
en tus ansias.
Y el niño,
el niño que levanta las manos
hacia el alba, saldrá indemne.

Afuera

La canción de R., I

El Hospital Central es mi nueva morada:
voy por sus corredores
con mi sol azotado.
Veo que hay enfermeras y gruesos camilleros
rumbo a la sombra de la esperanza
a ver qué pasa con la vida.
Veo que hay perchas taciturnas
y anhelantes de las camisas
y del polvo de los pobres.
Mi Amada duerme en la modesta cama.
Quiere llevármela la muerte,
pero yo la protejo con las manos violetas
de la pura virtud, de la ansiosa verdad,
de aquella que ha nombrado las piedras necesarias.
Me la quiere llevar,
pero yo no estoy solo:
cada baldosa me ayuda a estar de pie

and so you raise your voice to scare them away,
but they go on with their task:
they start on the radio, the mirrors,
the ruins of your sighs,
and the smoke of your poems.
There are days when nothing stops them
and with their wings they assault
us till they clean us out—you, me—
of everything that is dirty and that dreams.

Afuera

THE PARTY'S OUTSIDE

Whack the piñata
with your little doubts:
just like from a flower there will erupt
patriotic words that announce the Word;
from its belly, the talcum powder will burst
onto your anxieties.
And the child
—the child who raises his hands,
toward the dawn—will come out unhurt.

Afuera

I

Central Hospital is my new home:
I go down its halls
with my sun utterly thrashed.
I see nurses and husky stretcher bearers
on their way to the shadow of hope
to see what's happening with life.
I see silent clothes hangers
yearning for shirts
and for dust from the poor.
My sweetheart sleeps on a modest bed.
Death wants to take her from me,
but with purple hands of pure virtue,
I protect her from the anxious truth,
the one that has named the necessary stones.
It wants to take her from me,
but I'm not alone:
every floor tile helps me remain standing

y en cada espejo de la noche
mi corazón es una luna transparente.
Yo la protejo con la llama verde de los arcángeles
y de las hojas que nacen porque yo las ansío,
porque hay polleras y zapatos que son
ventanas, nubes, de amarla tanto.
Afuera está lloviendo hoy 15 de septiembre.

La canción de R

XXI

Respira el alba porque camina
suavemente hacia tus manos el viento.
En pañales, el día,
gatea por las orillas de los corazones.
Callados gatos regresan a los espejos.
Cuatro o cinco alfileres bostezan
y los ficheros amarillos,
como siempre,
arrugan la luna en los cajones.
No siempre faroles habrá
que limpien su barriga en el rocío,
pero hoy
todos en esta cuadra te soñaron
y preñados despiertan
de la tristeza
que en los zaguanes,
apretando parejas,
se descubre la frente.
Yo voy rumbo al trabajo,
hiriendo levemente el horizonte.

La canción de R.

LOS MUCHACHOS PERDIDOS

A los hermanos de
Juan Arrom y Anuncio Martí

No los busquen por los pasillos de los ministerios.
No pregunten a la policía:
Un comisario tiene la amnesia de los ministros
y su olor, su peso en coimas.

and in every mirror of night
my heart is a transparent moon.
I protect her with the green flame of archangels
and of blossoming leaves because I await them,
because there are skirts and shoes that are
windows, clouds, so much do I love her.
Outside it's raining today, September 15.

The Song of R,

XXI

The dawn breathes because the wind
moves softly toward your hands.
The day, still in diapers,
crawls through the edges of hearts.
Silent cats return to the mirrors.
Four or five brooches yawn
and the yellow file cabinets,
as always,
wrinkle the moon in their drawers.
There won't always be street lamps
cleaning their bellies on the dew,
but today
on this block they all dreamed of you
and, bulging, they awaken
from the sadness
that shows its forehead
as it catches couples,
in doorways.
I'm on my way to work,
lightly wounding the horizon.

The Song of R

THE LOST KIDS

To the brothers of
Juan Arrom and Anuncio Martí

Don't search for them in the halls of the ministries.
Don't ask the police:
A commissioner has a minister's amnesia
and his smell, his weight in bribes.

No aturdan con sus quejas al señor diputado
porque ocupado está en la dieta.
No se metan con Mauchi: no ven que está bebido.
No digan nada más que nada importa más
que verlos con la vida puesta
sobre los hombros.
Miremos hacia el cielo y salgamos a las calles.
¡Salgamos a las calles!

Afuera

Don't bewilder Mr. Representative with your complaints
because he's busy with his diet.
Don't get involved with Mauchi; can't you see he's drunk?
Don't say anything else, because nothing is more important
than seeing them shoulder
life on their own.
Let's look toward heaven and get out on the streets.
Let's get out on the streets!

Afuera

CARLOS VILLAGRA MARSAL

EL DESTERRADO

Yo necesito
volver allá,
donde colman de duelo
el cuenco de las madres,
donde llenan de sal nuestras heridas.

Tengo que regresar.
A mi tierra,
donde saquean el agua a los secanos,
donde demarcan las hambres
con alambres de púa.

De vuelta debo estar.

En mi tierra,
donde unos pocos mandan,
en tanto que en sus ojos le relucen las armas,
cuando a los demás sólo nos queda
sangre sajada en las espaldas
y sed amordazada
y rabia.

Precisamente quiero
volver allá,
porque todos sabemos
que cuanto más ciega sea
la sombra que soporta la patria,
más cercano estará,
a punto de asomarse
el resplandor seguro,
el goce incontenible de la madrugada.

Guaranía del desvelado

THE EXILED ONE

I need
to return there
where they heap mourning
into the cupped hands of mothers,
where they fill our wounds with salt.

I have to return.
to my land,
where they steal water from barren plains,
where they stake out hunger
with barbed wire.

I should be back there

On my land,
where just a few are in charge,
while their weapons shine in their eyes,
while the rest of us only have
blood cut out of our backs
and muzzled thirst
and rage.

Precisely, I want
to return there,
because we all know
that the darker the shadow
the country endures,
the closer will be
—about to appear—
the secure splendor,
the irrepressible joy of a new day.

Guaranía del desvelado

VARIACIONES EN DOS CLAVES

para una música inmediata de Sila Godoy

AQUEL HUMO

Quemazón azul
de octubre
veladura repujada
estás más cerca
de mi palabra
que del horizonte viejo.

Pilar de humareda capital
soy tu trasunto
una refracción apenas
de tu empeño:
brasa dispuesta
rojizo lenguaje codicioso
luego morosa vehemencia
niebla seca
ciego ascenso
y al fin disgregación
en el ensimismado
firmamento.

El júbilo difícil

EXPLICACIÓN DE UNA LLUVIA

y esperábamos,
pausa esmerilada,
ciudadela instantánea,
muralla tras muralla levantada
de arriba para abajo.

Con igual desdén
anulas
la llanura rumbosa
y la verde altanería de las piedras.

Goteadora, te atienden
los cocoteros desatados,
las aves estrictas en el monte.

VARIATIONS IN TWO KEYS

for an immediate music of Sila Godoy

THAT SMOKE

A blue burning
of October
a repoussé glaze,
you are closer
to my word
than to the old horizon.

A pillar of notable, dense smoke
I am your transcription
hardly a refraction
of your tenacity:
a willing ember
a burning red, ambitious language
then, a delinquent vehemence
dry mist
blind ascendance
and finally a dispersion
in the self-absorbed
firmament.

El júbilo difícil

EXPLANATION OF A RAIN SHOWER

and we awaited you,
a polished pause,
an instant citadel,
wall after wall built
from top down.

With equal disdain
you annul
the sumptuous plain
and the green arrogance of the stones.

Drizzle, awaiting you are
the unrestrained coconut palms
the stringent birds in the forest.

Y el joven viento norte
dibuja una canción que te enardece.

No obstante, enseguida resultas
garúa entrefina,
cerrazón,
soledad movediza.

Al cabo
escampas.

. . . Ya eres agua anterior, pero me dejas
indemne, cristalino,
y acribillado de ágiles certezas.

para J.A. Rauskin

El júbilo difícil

LOS ESPECTROS DIURNOS

Hay veces
en que la mañana se inmuta
y franquea o atranca un portalón translúcido
intermitentemente
sin otro fragor que el del azul concreto
arriba
de la abrasada tosca
de cúspides y graderías.

Una sombra desazonadora
rueda de por sí
se abate sube como pestaña ilusoria
pretende trocar el orden
de la inveterada travesía.

Por un rato
se guarecen los árboles
atrás de sus hojas
y hasta el fulgor justiciero
se coloca de canto en el tiempo
amonedando un oro bajo
a toda prisa.

Se trata a mi juicio
de nuestros muertos perfectamente vanos

And the young north wind
sketches a song that inflames you.

Nevertheless, you soon become
a very fine drizzle,
a blanket of storm clouds,
a movable solitude.

In the end
you abate.

. . . no longer are you water
but you leave me undamaged, crystalline
and riddled with agile certainties.

for J.A. Rauskin

El júbilo difícil

DIURNAL SPECTRES

There are times
when the morning looks worried
and passes through or bolts shut a translucent gateway
intermittently
with no other clamor than that of blue concrete
above
the heated tuff
of peaks and plateaus.

An irritating shadow,
rolls by, dives
and climbs like an illusory eyelash
it wants to change the order
of the long-established crossing.

For a moment
the trees take shelter
behind their leaves
and even the severe brilliance
gets placed on edge in time
minting twelve-carat gold
in all haste.

In my judgment, it's about
our perfectly vain, dearly departed,

cuya soledad compacta
apreciaría
alternar con las del cielo habitual.

Empero estos sucesos
no duran el minuto que se gasta en nombrarlos:
presto la mañana
torna a singlar
legítima
incorrupta
proa insignia
hacia su naufragio personal
en el mediodía.

Para Carlos Germán Belli

El júbilo difídil

ACOMETIDA DEL TAGUATO'I*

Con el silencio violento
de tu penacho azulejo
hincas y ejerces un viejo
embate oblicuo en el viento;
un choque, un destello hambriento
bastan: la sangre despena
tu sed, el aire refrena
su ardor o su sobresalto
y un vago plumón en alto
declara la muerte ajena.

para Francisco Madariaga

* Gavilán-chico o Esparvero: *Accipiterstriatus (Accipitrídea)*

El júbilo difícil

CANTO FIEL DEL MASAKARAGUA'I*

Nueve sílabas veloces
infundes, congregas, sueñas
de la fronda que desdeñas
hasta el resol que conoces;
honra de las otras voces,
fiesta de alhaja temprana,

whose compact loneliness
would appreciate
changing places with those of their usual heaven.

But these events
don't endure even for the minute it takes to name them:
swiftly the morning
returns to sailing
legitimately,
incorruptly,
its flagged bow
toward its personal shipwreck
at midday.

For Carlos Germán Belli

El júbilo difícil

ATTACK OF THE TAGUATO'I*

With the violent silence
of your bluish crest
you thrust and exercise an ancient,
oblique attack in the wind;
a crash, a hungry spark
are enough: blood relieves
your thirst, the air restrains
your shock or your ardor
and a vague feather up high
declares the death of another.

for Francisco Madariaga

*Sparrow hawk: Accipiterstriatus (Accipitridea)

El júbilo difícil

FAITHFUL SONG OF THE MASAKARAGUA'I*

Nine speedy syllables
you instill, you assemble, you dream
of the foliage that you disdain
and the sun's glare that you know;
honor of other voices,
fiesta of an early jewel,

tan liberal como ufana
tu música condesciende
y nítidamente aprende
nutre y salva la mañana.

para Emilio Pérez Chaves

* *Troglodytes aedon (Troglodytídea)*

El júbilo difícil

ARASA PYTÂ*
Una luz permisiva,
cimera, oronda,
tu madurez sostiene,
tus perfumes adorna.

Zarcillo del verano
y juntadora
de zumbos, de gorjeos
que apetecen tu forma.

Esta virtud de enero
calma la boca;
toda mi infancia cabe
en tu médula roja.

Latir de la inocencia
o de otras cosas:
palpo tu piel y entiendo
la sumergida historia.

Candela del guayabo
ingente y poca:
el conjuro no basta,
su jarabe me sobra.

para Francisco Pérez-Maricevich

*Guayaba-roja: *Psidium pommiferum Mirtácea*

El júbilo difícil

as liberal as you are proud
your music yields
and neatly teaches,
nourishes and saves the morning.

for Emilio Pérez Chaves

*Troglodytes aedon (Troglodytidea)

El júbilo difícil

RED GUAVA*

A permissive light,
at its peak, conceited,
sustains your ripeness,
adorns your perfumes.

Tendril of the summer
and gatherer
of the buzzing and warbling
that crave your form.

This virtue of January
calms the mouth;
all my infancy fits
in your red marrow.

A throb of innocence
or of other things;
I touch your skin and understand
your submerged history.

Light of the guava tree,
enormous and yet little:
the incantation isn't enough,
your sweet sap is too much.

For Francisco Pérez-Maricevich

*Red guava: *Psidium pommiferum Mirtácea)*

El júbilo difícil

EL GRITO EN LAS CALLES, I

Aquel grito detenido
tanto tiempo entre los dientes,
se arrojó a ganar la calle,
rompió las cuatro paredes.
Una garganta esparcida
le congrega y le sostiene
como un ardoroso escudo
entre el aire y nuestra gente.

Cuando el grito se corona
de libertad por la frente,
echan luz hasta las piedras,
los árboles se conmueven.

Grito que empieza en la tierra,
que el alba empuja y promete,
le defienden nuestros muertos,
le alimentan nuestros héroes.

La sangre es empuñadura
del grito que el pueblo atiende,
y si la sangre se afirma
las viejas sombras se pierden.

Asunción, ciudad vacía,
cansada de tanta peste,
te irá limpiando este río
cuanto más crezca y resuene.

Asunción, ciudad callada,
escucha cómo florece
el grito que está cambiando
tus esquinas y tu suerte.

para Gloria y Humberto Rubin

LAS SOMBRAS POR LA TIERRA, II

Tierra malaventurada
y huérfana de sus hijos,
mansión de la desmemoria
y del castigo.

THE SCREAMING IN THE STREETS, I

That prolonged scream
clenched so long in their teeth,
expelled, overcoming the street,
it knocked down the four walls.
A jovial throat
gathers it in and sustains it
like an ardent shield
between the air and our people.

When the cry is crowned
with liberty upon its head,
even stones emit light,
even trees are excited.

A cry that begins on earth,
that the dawn pushes and promises,
our dead defend it,
our heroes nourish it.

Blood is the sword hilt
of the shout that the people await,
and if blood stands fast
the old shadows get lost.

Asunción, empty city,
tired of so much plague,
this river will cleanse you
the more it grows and resounds.

Asunción, quiet city,
listen how the shouting
grows, changing
your street corners and your fate.

for Gloria and Humberto Rubin

SHADOWS ON THE LAND, II

Ill-fated land,
orphaned by your children,
mansion of forgetfulness
and of punishment.

Clavada a su sol desierto,
barrida por su destino,
crujen sus oscuros duelos
bajo los signos.

Para más, venden las aguas
ladrones recién venidos,
trozan los profundos árboles,
queman los trinos.

Y así la tierra que aguanta
la seca como el granizo,
no da siquiera una sombra
al desvalido.

Ya es hora, tierra, que salves
tus suaves panales íntimos
y ocultes tu azul pujante
del enemigo.

Forja tu niebla sagrada,
urde tu furor nutricio:
vuelve a ser la madre intensa
del campesino.

para Roberto Fernández Retamar

El júbilo difícil

Stuck in a desert sun,
swept by its destiny,
its obscure sorrows creak
under the signs.

Not only that, now thieves come
selling the water,
cutting deep forests into logs,
and burning the birds' warbling.

And so, the land that endures
drought as well as hail,
casts not even a shadow
on the helpless.

Now is the time, dear land, that you save
your soft, intimate honeycombs
and you hide your vigorous blue
from the enemy.

Forge your sacred mist,
plan your nourishing furor:
become again the intense mother
of the peasant.

for Roberto Fernández Retamar

El júbilo difícil

THE POETS AND THEIR BIBLIOGRAPHIES

All references to *ABC Color, La Nación*, *Noticias* and *Última Hora* pertain to newspapers published in Asunción, Paraguay. Some of the books listed below can be accessed (in Spanish only) at this website: http://www.cervantesvirtual.com/.

* * * * * * *

JOSÉ-LUIS APPLEYARD

Born and reared in Asunción, José Luis Appleyard (1927-1997) finished his high school education in Buenos Aires before returning to Asunción to complete a law degree at the Universidad Nacional de Asunción. He practiced law for a decade before becoming a journalist, and for years he posted a well-known column for *La Tribuna* entitled "Monólogos," as well as serving as a book reviewer and director of cultural supplements. Afterwards, he wrote a column for the afternoon daily *Última Hora*. He was a member and secretary of the Academia Paraguaya de la Lengua (The Paraguayan Academy of Language) and former president of the Paraguayan PEN Club. In 1997, Appleyard received the National Literary Award for his poetry.

POETRY

Poesía de la Academia Universitaria. Asunción: Author's ed., 1953.

Entonces era siempre. Asunción: Trapiche, 1963.

El sauce permanece y tres motivos. Asunción: Péndulo, 1965.

Tomado de la mano. Asunción: NAPA, 1981.

El labio y la palabra. Asunción: La República, 1982.

Solamente los años. Asunción: Alcándara, 1983.

La voz que nos hablamos. Asunción: El Lector, 1983.

Las palabras secretas. Asunción: El Lector, 1988.

Desde el tiempo que vivo. Asunción: Comuneros, 1993.

José-Luis Appleyard. Antología Poética. Ed. Fernando Pistilli. Asunción: El Lector, 1996.

Las cenizas de la vida. Asunción: Fernando Pistilli Miranda, 1997.

Poesía [Homenaje de la Sociedad de Escritores de Paraguay]. Asunción: Sociedad de Escritores de Paraguay, 2002.

CRITICISM, REVIEWS, INTERVIEWS

Acosta, Delfina, "Poesía, mística, plural y bella." *Suplemento Cultural* (*ABC Color*) 20 Apr. 2003: 4.

Appleyard, José Luis. "Veo con dolor el rostro de la corrupción en todas partes." Interview with Victorio Suárez V. *Literatura paraguaya (1900-2000)*. By Victorio Suárez V. Asunción: Servilibro, 2001. 261-267.

Delgado, Susy. "José-Luis Appleyard, el silencio y las lámparas." *Cultural* (*La Nación*), 22 Feb. 1998: 1; 7.

---. "José-Luis Appleyard, el poeta de un tiempo que era siempre." *Cultural* (*La Nación*), 14 Feb. 1999: 3-5.

---. *25 nombres capitales de la literatura paraguaya*. Ed. Susy Delgado. Asunción: Servilibro, 2005.

Rodríguez-Alcalá, Hugo. "Lírica juvenil de bardos viejos: José Luis Appleyard." 127-132; "Federico García Lorca y poetas paraguayos." 29-33. *Poetas paraguayos y otros breves ensayos*. Asunción: Intercontinental, 1988.

Romero, Elvio. "José-Luis Appleyard." *Correo Semanal* (*Última Hora*) 27 Dec. 1997: 14.

Vallejos, Roque. "Omnipresencia de la poesía de José-Luis Appleyard." *José-Luis Appleyard, Antología Poética*. Ed. Fernando Pistilli. Asunción: El Lector, 1996.

---. "La poesía de Jose-Luis Appleyard." *Correo Semanal* (*Última Hora*) 15 June 1996: 12-13.

* * * * * * *

MONCHO AZUAGA

Moncho Azuaga (Asunción, 1953-), is a poet, dramatist, and narrator when he's not working as a lawyer. Founding member of the Manuel Ortiz Guerrero poetry workshop, (a community of poets of the Paraguayan "Generation of 1980,") the Centro Paraguayo de Teatro, the Society of Paraguayan Writers, and has been a member of the governing board of the PEN Club of Paraguay. His litarary work has been awarded prizes and recognition on eight occasions in national and international competitions, and his short stories and poems have appeared in various national anthologies. Azuaga is perhaps best known for his novel, *Celda 12* (1991), denouncing human rights violations during the Stroessner regime, and his prodigious work in both writing and directing popular theater productions for poor urban and rural communities in Paraguay. In 2004-2005 he participated in the human rights campaign, "Paraguay: No Excuses for Poverty."

POETRY

(with Jorge Aymar Vargas.) *Jirones de espera*. Asunción: Arte Nuevo, 1981.

Bajo los vientos del sur. Asunción: Alcándara, 1986.

Ciudad sitiada. Asunción: Karand'y, 1989.

"Chiapas." *Suplemento Cultural* (*ABC Color*) 23 Jan. 1994: 1.

"Los degollados." *Nexo* (Asunción) 10 Nov. 1995: 13.

CRITICISM, REVIEWS, INTERVIEWS

Amaral, Raúl, et. al. "Moncho Azuaga." *Forjadores del Paraguay. Diccionariobiográfico*. Buenos Aires: Quevedo, 2000. 59-60.

Azuaga, Moncho and Emilio Lugo. "Literatura paraguaya de hoy: Una entrevista con dos escritores paraguayos: Moncho Azuaga y Emilio Lugo." Interview with Wolfgang Lustig. Asunción: 14 Oct. 1992. <http://www.staff.uni-ainz.de/lustig/texte/lustig_Azuaga.pdf#search='Moncho%20Azuaga'>

---. "El poder es corrupto y emana impunidad." Interview with Victorio Suárez V. *Literatura paraguaya (1900-2000)*. By Victorio Suárez V. Asunción: Servilibro, 2001. 387-394.

Haladyna, Ronald. "Una inmovilización poética: *Ciudad sitiada* de Moncho Azuaga." *Cultura* (*La Nación*) 5 Oct. 1997: 3-5.

* * * * * * *

GLADYS CARMAGNOLA

One of Paraguay's most prolific poets, Gladys Carmagnola (Guarambaré, Paraguay 1939-), first published poems in local newspapers in1960. In addition to many honorable mentions and first place awards from the Association of Art Critics and Commentators of Miami (1985), she has received the Silver Award of the Premio del Ateneo de Cultura Popular, (Córdoba, Spain, 1989), and four national literary awards, including the prestigious Municipal Award for Literature in 1996. Her poems have been included in several international anthologies and have been translated to Portuguese, English, French, and Italian.

Most of Carmagnola's life has revolved around literature: she is a member of the Pen Club of Paraguay, as well as the Association of Paraguayan Writers, the co-founder of the Society of Writers of Paraguay and of the Associated Paraguayan Female Writers. Ms. Carmagnola has participated in numerous poetry workshops at the Universidad Católica and the Universidad Nacional, and has participated in numerous literary juries. She has also taught languages and communication in secondary schools; has written various books of poetry for children; edited *Tu beso es muchedumbre* (an homage to Paraguayan writer Josefina Plá); founded a reading club for girls in the town of Luque; and developed a series of Saturday morning poetry conclaves, inviting Paraguayan poets to talk about their works. For Gladys Carmagnola's considerable contributions to the development of cultural activities, she was awarded an honorable recognition by Paraguay's House of Representatives of the Republic of Paraguay in June, 2009, and two awards for thirty years of meritorious service to the Universidad Católica in 2010.

POETRY

Ojitos negros. [Children's poetry.] Asunción: EMASA, 1965.

Piolín. [Children's poetry.] Luque, Paraguay: Author's edition, 1979. Republished in a supplement, *El Diario Noticias* 1979; 2nd ed. 1985; 3rd ed. Asunción: Alfaguara / Santillana, 2008.

Navidad. [Children's poetry] Asunción: Author's edition, 1966; 2nd ed. Asunción: El Arte, 1980.

Cecilia. Asunción: Author's edition, 1982.

Lazo esencial. Asunción: El Corcel, 1982; 2nd ed. Asunción: El Corcel, 1995.

A la intemperie. Asunción: Alcándara, 1984; 2nd ed. El Corcel, 1998.

Igual que en las capueras. Asunción: CEPUC, 1989.

Un poquito más allá. Asunción: Author's edition, 1989.

Depositaria infiel. Asunción: CEPUC, 1992.

Un sorbo de agua fresca. Asunción: CEPUC, 1995. 2nd. ed. CEPUAC, 1996.

Territorio esmeralda. Asunción: Intercontinental, 1997.

Un verdadero hogar (1960-1967). Asunción: El Corcel, 1998.

Banderas y señales. Asunción: El Corcel, 1999.

Lunas de harina. [Children's poetry.] Asunción: FEDIPO, 1999.

Río Blanco y antiguo. Asunción: Intercontinental, 2002.

¿Paseo--¿ al zoo? --¡Lógico! [Children's poetry.] Asunción: Intercontinental, 2003.

Una rosa de hierro. Asunción: El Corcel, 2005.

Poema de la celebración. Asunción: Arandurã, 2005.

Crónicas de cualquierparte. Asunción: Piolín, 2008.

Yo quiero ser. [Children's poetry.] Asunción: Alfaguara / Santillana, 2008.

¿De lodo, miel y lágrimas? Asunción: Arandurã, 2010. (Finalist in the Fernando Rielo Mystical Poetry Award, Madrid Spain, 2008.)

CRITICISM, REVIEWS, INTERVIEWS

Acosta, Delfina. Rev. of *A la intemperie* and *Lazo esencial*, by Gladys Carmagnola. *Nosotras* (*ABC Color*): 11 May 1989: 3.

Appleyard, José Luis. Rev. of *Piolín*. "Realmente para niños." *La Tribuna Cultura* 7 Dec. 1979: 16.

---. Rev. of *Lazo esencial*. "*Lazo esencial* de Gladys Carmagnola." *Cultura* (*La Tribuna*) 30 Jan. 1982: 4.

Barreto, Maribel. "Del poema al poemario. Gladys Carmagnola (con motivo del 40 aniversario de su primer poemario)". *Revista del PEN Club, Paraguay* 4.12 (Dec. 2006): 76-89.

Carmagnola, Gladys. "Gladys Carmagnola, poetisa: Empeñarse en el fuego de la palabra." Interview with César González. *Correo Semanal* 23 May 1992: 22.

---. "En este tercermundismo todo es muy difícil." Interview with Victorio Suárez. *Suplemento Cultural* (*ABC Color*) 7 Dec.1993: 2-3.

---. "Gladys Carmagnola: Diálogo con la poesía." Interview with Elsa Troche. *Revista* (*Noticias*) 31 Jan. 1993: 22-23.

---. "Las Razones del corazón." Interview with Milia Gayoso. *El Séptimo Día* 2 July 1995: 4-5.

---. Interview. "Gladys Carmagnola: Vivir en la poesía." *Revista* (*Noticias*) 9 July 1995. 40.

---. Interview. "Ida y vuelta: Gladys Carmagnola." *Revista* (*ABC Color*) 10 Dec. 1995: 3.

---. "Poetisa y poeta." Interview with Delfina Acosta. *Revista* (*ABC Color*): 21 Apr. 1996. 11.

---. Interview. "Más agua para su cántaro." *La Nación* 24 Oct. 1996.

---. "La entrega total a la palabra." Interview with Ruth González. *La Mujer* (*Ultima Hora*) 15 Mar. 1997: 42.

---. Interview. "La poesía, una forma de vivir." *Revista Jazmín* Apr. 1997: 10-12.

---. Interview. "Gladys Carmagnola de Medina, o la poesía de la cotidianeidad." *Suplemento de Cultura* (*Noticias*) 6 Dec. 1998: 4.

---. "Poesía que fluye." Interview with Lourdes Peralta. *Nosotras* (*ABC Color*) 6 June 2002: 1.

---. "*Río Blanco y antiguo* de Gladys Carmagnola." Interview with Delfina Acosta. *Suplemento Cultural* (*ABC Color*) 9 June 2002: 4.

---. "Gladys Carmagnola; Crónicas de Cualquierparte." *ABC Digital* 6 June 2008: <http://archivo.abc.com.py/2008-06-01/articulos/420215/gladys-carmagnola-cronicas-de-cualquierparte>

"La casa incendiada en el territorio esmeralda." Rev. of *Territorio Esmeralda*, by Gladys Carmagnola. *Correo Semanal* (*Ultima Hora*) 15 Mar. 1997: 8.

"Unas crónicas para descubrir y conocer." Rev. of *Crónicas de cualquier parte*, by Gladys Carmagnola *Artes y Espectáculos* (*Ultima Hora*) 13 Dec. 2009: 62.

Delgado, Susy. "Gladys Carmagnola, una poetisa frente al futuro." *Cultural* (*La Nación*) 8 Feb. 1998: 3-5.

Gamarra Doldan, Pedro. "La Revolución de 1947 en la poesía paraguaya: En torno al último libro de Gladys Carmagnola." Rev. of *El territorio esmeralda*, by Gladys Carmagnola. *Noticias* 22 June 1997: 4.

"Gladys Carmagnola: Una depositaria infiel fiel a su poesía." Rev. of *Una depositaria infiel*, by Gladys Carmagnola. *Suplemento Femenino* (*Última Hora*) 22 Sept. 1992: 9.

"Gladys Carmagnola y tres nuevos–viejos libros." *Suplemento Cultural* (*ABC Color*) 24 Jan. 1999: 1.

Haladyna, Ronald. "*A la intemperie* de Gladys Carmagnola." *Cultura* (*La Nación* 24 Aug.1997: 2-3.

Pla, Josefina. "Voces femeninas en la poesía paraguaya." *Suplemento Cultural* (*ABC*) 19 Dec. 1982: 7.

---. Rev. of *Depositaria infiel*, by Gladys Carmagnola. *Suplemento Cultural* (*ABC*) 29 Nov. 1992: 4.

Rev. of *Lazo esencial*, by Gladys Carmagnola. *Suplemento Cultural* (*ABC Color*) 11 Apr. 1982: 7.

Rev. of *Igual que en las capueras*, by Gladys Carmagnola. *Suplemento Especial* (*ABC Color*) 7 Dec. 1989: 2.

Rodríguez-Alcalá, Hugo. "Sobre una embajadora del viento y de la lluvia." *Poetas y prosistas paraguayos y otros breves ensayos*. Asunción: Intercontinental, 1988. 181-185.

---. "Sobre *A la intemperie* de Gladys Carmagnola." *Poetas y prosistas paraguayos y otros breves ensayos.* Asunción: Intercontinental, 1988. 177-180.

---. "El sorbo de poesía de Gladys Carmagnola." Rev. of *Un sorbo de agua fresca*, by Gladys Carmagnola. *Arte y Espectáculos* (*La Nación*) 28 June 1995: 6.

Vallejos, Roque. Rev. of *Un sorbo de agua fresca*, by Gladys Carmagnola. *Última Hora* 30 Sept. 1995, 8.

* * * * * * *

SUSY DELGADO

Upon completion of her studies in communication at the Universidad Nacional de Asunción and at the Universidad Complutense de Madrid in 1979, Susy Delgado (San Lorenzo, Paraguay, 1949-) began work as a journalist for various newspapers in Asunción: La Tribuna, La Tarde, Hoy, and La Nación. She also studied modern dance for many years in Buenos Aires, Madrid and London.

As is often the case for writers in Latin America, she has worked in a variety of media, writing screen plays for films and television as well as commercial copy for several publicity firms; translating Guaraní for the Marandú Applied Anthropology Project; and directing cultural programs for various cultural centers in the capital. During the 1990s, she was the director of the supplement *Cultural* of *La Nación*, a daily newspaper of Asunción, and in 2002 she published *La sangre florecida*, a book of short stories. As a strong proponent of her bilingual culture, she has published bilingual books of her own poetry, has edited anthologies of Paraguayan poets and children's stories in Guaraní and Spanish, has represented Paraguay in various indigenous and bilingual conferences in Europe and the Americas, and has been instrumental in promoting bilingualism in national legislation.

Susy Delgado has received the following awards for her published works: Premio de Amigos del Arte; Premio Radio Curupayty, Premio de la Junta Municipal de Asunción; and was a finalist in the Premio Especial de Literaturas Indígenas de Casa de las Américas, Cuba. Her poems have also appeared in numerous literary journals and several collective anthologies of Paraguayan poetry.

POETRY

Algún extraviado temblor. Asunción: El Lector, 1986.

Tesarái mboyve / Antes del olvido. Trans. Carlos Villagra Marsal and Jacobo Rauskin. Asunción: Alcándara, 1987.

El patio de los duendes. Asunción: Arandurã, 1991.

Tataypýpe. Junto al fuego. (Bilingual ed.) Asunción: Arandurã, 1992.

Sobre el beso del viento. Asunción: Arandurã, 1995.

La rebelión de papel. Asunción: Arandurã and Colihue-Mimbipa, 1996.

Tatypype. 3rd ed. (Trilingual ed.: Guaraní-Spanish-English.) Trans. Susy Delgado, Susan Smith Nash. Asunción: Arandurã , 1998.

Ayvu membyre / Hijo de aquel verbo. (Bilingual ed.: Guaraní-Spanish.) Trans. Susy Delgado. Asunción: Arandurã, 1999.

Ayvu membyre / Hijo de aquel verbo / Offspring of the Distant Word. (Trilingual ed.: Guaraní-Spanish-English.) Trans. Susy Delgado, Susan Smith Nash. Asunción: Arandurã, 2001.

Antología primeriza. Asunción: Arandurã, 2001.

Las últimas hogueras. Asunción: Arandurã, 2003. *Ñe'ẽ saraki, textos en castellano y guaraní*. Asunción: Servilibro, 2003. *Ñe'ẽ jovái (Palabra en dúo.)* (Bilingual anthology with commentary by Carlos Villagra Marsal, Bartomeu Meliá, Víctor Casartelli, Susan Smith Nash, Wolf Lustig, Tracy Lewis, Martín Alvarenga, José Alberto de la Fuente y Carla Fernandes.) Asunción: Arandurã, 2005.

Jevy ko'ẽ (Día del regreso), cuentos y poemas bilingües. Asunción: Arandurã, 2007.

Tyre'y rape (Camino del huérfano.) (Bilingual poems.) Asunción: Arandurã, 2008.

Xestado na palabra (Ayvu membyre). (Bilingual ed.: Guaraní-Galician.) Trans. and Intro. Fátima Rodríguez. La Coruña, Spain: Espiral Maior, 2008.

Ogue jave Takuapu / Cuando se apaga el Takua. (Bilingual ed.) Asunción: Arandurã, 2010. This book is accessible online: http://www.portalguarani.com/obras_autores_detalles.php?id_obras=13468

CRITICISM, REVIEWS, INTERVIEWS

Acosta, Delfina. "La voz profunda de Susy Delgado." *ABC Color, SuplementoCultural* 12 Aug. 2001: 2-3.

Andreu, Jean. "Literatura paraguaya actual." *Caravelle : Cahiers du Monde Hispanique et Luso-Brasilien.* Toulouse, France: Université de Toulouse 58 (1992): 169-195.

Bareiro Saguier, Rubén. "Prólogo-Carta." Susy Delgado. *Antología primeriza.* Asunción: Arandurã, 2001. 9-11.

Fernandes, Carla. "En el principio de la poesía está el mito. Rev. of *Ayvu membyre* (*Hijo De aquel verbo*), and *Ñe'ẽ jovái* (*Palabra en dúo*)," by Susy Delgado. Asunción: Arandurã. 56-66.

Fuente, José Alberto de la. "Susy Delgado: Un puente entre la historia y la memoria." *ABC Color, Suplemento Cultural* 24 Feb. 2002: 2-3.

González Real, Osvaldo. "La rebelión de papel: La poesía contestataria de Susy Delgado." *Antología primeriza.* By Susy Delgado. Asunción: Arandurã, 2001. 27-29.

Haladyna, Ronald. "Palpando *Un extraviado temblor* de Susy Delgado." *Crítica* (Asunción) 8.13 (1997): 75-77. Reprinted: *Antología primeriza.* By Susy Delgado. Asunción: Arandurã, 2001. 19-24.

Lewis, Tracy. "Epistemología paraguaya: La palabra-fuego en la poesía de Susy Delgado." Unpublished paper. Las Vegas, Nevada: Congress of Latin-American Studies Association, Oct. 2004.

Lustig, Wolfgang. "A modo de introducción." *Poesía paraguaya de ayer y de hoy*. Vol. 2. Asunción: Intercontinental, 1997. 43.

---. "*Versos del fuego*. Breve introducción al universo poético de Susy Delgado." *Tesarái mboyve (El fuego y la palabra)* and *Ñe'ë jovái* (*Palabra en dúo*)," by Susy Delgado. Asunción: Arandurã, 2005.

Madariaga, Francisco. "Sobre el *Beso del viento* de Susy Delgado." *Antología primeriza*. By Susy Delgado. Asunción: Arandurã, 2001. 25-26.

Meliá, Bartomeu. "La lengua guaraní del Paraguay." *Colecciones MAPFRE* (Madrid, Spain)1992: 229-230.

---. "*Tataypype*, el fuego y la palabra." *Tesarái mboyve. (El fuego y la palabra.) Ñe'ë jovái* [*Palabra en dúo*]," by Susy Delgado. Asunción: Arandurã, 2005. 14-16.

Roa Bastos, Augusto. "Conocimiento de la poesía." *Antología primeriza*. By Susy Delgado. Asunción: Arandurã, 2001. 12-18.

Villagra Marsal, Carlos. "En torno a *Tesarái mboyve*." *Tesarái mboyve. (El fuego y la palabra.) Ñe'ë jovái* (*Palabra en dúo*)," by Susy Delgado. Asunción: Arandurã, 2005. 13.

* * * * * * *

OSCAR FERREIRO

Author of over forty books published in Paraguay and abroad, Oscar Ferreiro (Villa del Pilar, Paraguay, 1927-Asunción, 2004) resided in San Lorenzo, outside of Asunción. He made his living as a surveyor and agronomist, but he made his name as a poet, dramatist, essayist and as a notable translator, especially of French poetry. He was one of the very few writers who represented avant-garde and surrealist tendencies in his country. Although his literary production was not prolific, it was important, and he has been included among a well-known group of poets known as the "Generation of 1940." Ferreiro died on July 31, 2004 of complications following a long illness.

POETRY

Antología. Asunción: Alcándara, 1982.

El gallo de la alquería y otros compuestos. Asunción: Arte Nuevo, 1987.

Antología poética. Ed. and prologue, J.A. Rauskin. Asunción: El Lector, 1996.

CRITICISM , REVIEWS, INTERVIEWS

Acosta, Delfina. "El surrealismo en la poesía paraguaya y Oscar Ferreiro." *ABC Color Suplemento Cultural* 23 Feb. 2003: 4.

Centurión Morínigo, Ubaldo. *Poesía y ética de Oscar Ferreiro y otros temas*. Asunción: Author's edition, 2001.

Delgado, Susy. "Oscar Ferreiro es un poeta con las manos en la tierra." *Cultural* (*La Nación*) 15 June 2003: 18.

Ferreiro, Oscar. "La palabra de un grande." Interview with Mario Casartelli and Sergio Cáceres Mercado. *Correo Semanal* (*Última Hora*.) 18-19 Aug. 2001: 8-9.

---. "El cambio es una mentira en este proceso." Interview with Victorio Suárez V. *Literatura paraguaya (1900-2000)*. By Victorio Suárez V. Asunción: Servilibro, 2001. 251-254.

Rauskin, J. A. "Nota Preliminar: La poesía de Oscar Ferreiro." *Oscar Ferreiro. Antología Poética*. Ed. J.A. Rauskin. Asunción: El Lector, 1996. 7-10.

Rodríguez-Alcalá, Hugo. "Federico García Lorca y poetas paraguayos." *Poetas y prosistas paraguayos y otros breves ensayos*. Asunción: Intercontinental, 1988. 29-33.

* * * * * * *

RENÉE FERRER

Renée Ferrer (Asunción, 1944-) is one of Paraguay's most versatile and prolific writers. In addition to twenty-six books of poetry and anthologies (many of which have gone into multiple editions), she has published books of short stories, novels, plays, theater adaptations of her novels, and even a doctoral thesis in history. Her work has been translated to Guaraní, French, English, German, Swedish, Romanian, Portuguese, Italian, Bulgarian Arabic, and Albanian. She has won numerous national and international literary awards, and her poetry and stories have been included in national and international anthologies. Renée Ferrer resides in Asunción with her family.

POETRY

Hay surcos que no se llenan. Asunción: Author's ed., 1965.

Voces sin réplica. Asunción: Author's ed., 1967.

Cascarita de nuez. Aunción: Artes Gráficas Zamphirópolos, 1978.

Desde el cañadón de la memoria. Asunción: Escuela Técnica Salesiana, 1982. 2nd ed. Hamburg, Germany: Paul Molnar, 1984.

Galope. Asunción: Mediterráneo, 1985.

Campo y cielo. Asunción: Mediterráneo, 1985.

Peregrino de la eternidad. Sobreviviente. Asunción: Alcándara, 1985.

Nocturnos. Asunción: Arte Nuevo, 1987.

Sobreviviente. 2nd ed. Madrid: Torremozas, 1988.

Viaje a destiempo. Asunción: Universidad Católica Nuestra Señora de la Asunción, 1989.

De lugares, momentos e implicancias varias. Asunción: Ñandutí Vive / Intercontinental, 1990.

El acantilado y el mar. Asunción: Arandurã, 1992.

Itinerario del deseo. Asunción: Arandurã, 1994; 2nd ed. Asunción: Arandurã, 1995. 3rd ed. (Bilingual: Spanish-Portuguese), 1996.

La voz que me fue dada (Poesía 1965-1995). Asunción: Don Bosco, 1996.

El resplandor y las sombras. Asunción: Arandurã, 1996.

De la eternidad y otros delirios. Asunción: Intercontinental, 1997.

Desde el encendido corazón del monte. Ka'aguay pa'u rendy ruguaite guive. (Bilingual:Guaraní-Spanish.) Asunción: Intercontinental, 1998.

Survivor-Sobreviviente. (Spanish-English ed.) Trans. Glenda Richter, Ronald Haladyna. Asunción: Arandurã, 1999.

El ocaso del milenio. Asunción: El Corcel, 1999.

Poesía completa hasta el año 2000. Asunción: Arandurã, 2000.

Las cruces del olvido. Asunción: Intercontinental, 2001.

Itinerario del deseo—Itinerary of Desire. (Bilingual: Spanish-English.) Trans. Betsy Partyka. Asunción: Alta Voz, 2002.

Peregrino de la eternidad/Sobreviviente. (Bilingual: Spanish-English.) Trans. Tracy K. Lewis. Asunción: Alta Voz, 2005.

Celebración del cuerpo y otros cantos. Asunción: Arandurã, 2007.

Cascarita de nuez—Little Nutshell. (Bilingual: Spanish-English) Trans. Tracy K Lewis. Asunción: Fausto, 2007.

Las moradas del universo. Asunción: Servilibro, 2011.

CRITICISM, REVIEWS, INTERVIEWS

Acosta, Delfina. "Las cruces del olvido, nuevo poemario de Renée Ferrer." *Suplemento Cultural* (*ABC Color.*) 28 Oct. 2001: 2-3.

Bareiro Saguier, Rubén. "Prólogo." *Desde el cañadón de la memoria.* By Renée Ferrer. 2nd ed. Hamburg: R.F.A., 1984: 3-5.

Caballero Mora, Miguel. "Panorama de la literatura paraguaya actual." *Diario Noticias.* 15 Mar. 2002: 4.

"Cuando la palabra trae el signo del fuego. *Itinerario del deseo.*" *Cultura* (*Diario Noticias*) 25 Apr. 1995.

Delgado Costa, José. "Renée Ferrer con ojos humanos, punto. Tres vidas y una misma realidad." *Noticias* 25 Aug. 1996.

Delgado, Susy. "El deseo, desde el alma de una mujer." *Mundo del Libro.* Asunción: Arandurã Apr. 1995.

---. "Renée Ferrer y los porqués de nuestra literatura." *Cultural* (*LaNación*) 4 Feb. 1996.

---. "Renée Ferrer, los surcos distintos de algunas obsesiones." *Cultural* (*La Nación*) 18 July, 1999: 3-5.

---. "Renée Ferrer, después del Festival de Medellín." *Cultural* (*La Nación*), 24 June 2001: 3-4.

---. "Renée Ferrer, siembra y cosecha en los Estados Unidos." *Cultural* (*La Nación*) 10 Nov. 2002: 5.

Dionisi, María Gabriella. "El elemento musical en la obra de Renée Ferrer." *América Sin Nombre* (Valencia, Spain) Dec. 2002: 12-17.

Fernandes, Carla. "Renée Ferrer, una de las voces de la literatura paraguaya actual." *El Diario Noticias* 31 Aug. 1997: 2-3.

---. "Cuando la literatura rompe fronteras." *El Diario Noticias* 14 Sept. 1997: 4.

---. *Fronteras de la literatura paraguaya: La obra de Renée Ferrer*. Asunción: Arandurã, 2006.

Ferrer, Renée. "Renée Ferrer y Luis María Martínez hablan de literatura de compromiso." Interview with Delfina Acosta. *Suplemento Cultural* (*ABC Color*) 30 May 1999: 2-3.

---. "Desenmascarar la doble moral, la hipocresía." Interview with Victorio Suárez V. *Literatura paraguaya (1900-2000)*. By Victorio Suárez V. Asunción: Servilibro, 2001. 349-354.

---. "Conversaciones sabrosas." Interview with Lita Pérez Cáceres. *Viernes* (*Noticias*) 15 Mar. 2002: 4.

---. Interview with Xavier Oquendo Troncoso. Oct. 2007. http://elcuestionariodelescritor.blogspot.com/2007_10_01_archive.html

Franz, Thomas R. "Estudio Crítico." *Poesía completa hasta el año 2000*. By Renée Ferrer. Asunción: Arandurã 2000. 7-27.

González Real, Osvaldo. Prólogo. *Las moradas del universo*. By Renée Ferrer. Asunción: Servilibro, 2011.

Gorodischer, Angélica. "Morir detrás de las palabras." *Cultural* (*La Nación*) 14 May 2000: 1-2.

Haladyna, Ronald. "Las múltiples voces de *La voz que me fue dada*." *Cultural* (*La Nación*) 19 Oct. 1997: 3-5.

---. "El holocausto y los últimos poemas terrestres." *Sobreviviente/Survivor*. By Renée Ferrer. Asunción: Arandurã, 1998.

---. "El holocausto nuclear: Visiones poéticas de Renée Ferrer y Washington Benavides." *El Diario Noticias*. 5 Dec. 1999.

---. "La visión cosmológica en la poesía de Renée Ferrer. *Scriptura* (University of Lleida, Catalonia, Spain) 21-22: 2010: 309-317.

Heras, César Alonso de las. Prólogo. *Desde el cañadón de la memoria*. By Renée Ferrer. Asunción: Escuela Técnica Salesiana, 1982.

Ibargoyen, Saúl. "Poesía de Paraguay." *Tinta Seca, Revista de Arte y Literatura* (Morelos, Mexico) 2002: 62.

Izaguirre, Ester de. "Imagen y trascendencia de la obra poética de Renée Ferrer." *La voz que me fue dada*. By Renée Ferrer. Asunción: Don Bosco, 1995.

Kisil, André. "Garimpando a poesía de Renée Ferrer." O Escritor (São Paolo, Brazil) Feb.1996: 11.

Lewis, Tracy K. "Prefacio del Traductor." *Peregrino de la eternidad/ Sobreviviente*. By Renée Ferrer. Asunción: Alta Voz, 2005.

Partyka, Betsy. "An Intimate Journey through Renée Ferrer's *Itinerary of Desire*." by Renée Ferrer. Asunción: Alta Voz, 2002: 15-24.

---. "Una nueva generación de escritoras paraguayas rompe el silencio autoritario." *Cultural* (*La Nación*) 11 Feb. 2001: 1-3.

Peiró Barco, José Vicente. "Una pluma rebelde." *Correo Semanal* (*Última Hora*) 18-19 Aug. 2001: 18-19.

---. "Elvio Romero, Rubén Bareiro Saguier, Renée Ferrer, Jacobo Rauskin. Calas de la poesía paraguaya." *Dos orillas y un encuentro: La literatura paraguaya actual*. Ed. Mar Langa Pizarro. Alicante, Spain: Universidad de Alicante, 2006. 193-210.

Pérez Maricevich, Francisco. Prólogo. *Voces sin réplica*. By Renée Ferrer. Asunción: Author's ed., 1967.

Tone, José Luis de. "Incomunicación y liberación en una poética propuesta." *ABC Color* 13 Mar. 2002: 36.

Valdez, Edgar. "Dos mujeres ejemplares." *Última Hora* 9-10 Sept. 1995: 20-21.

---. "Renée Ferrer, una poetisa singular." *Correo Semanal* (*Ultima Hora*) 22 June 1996: 12-13.

---. "Renée Ferrer, poeta." *Correo Semanal* (*Última Hora*) 27-28 May 2000: 22-23.

---. "Canto al marzo paraguayo." *Correo Semanal* (*Última Hora*) 3-4 Nov., 2001: 18-19.

---. "Epica y lirismo en Renée Ferrer." *Correo Semanal* (*Última Hora*) 31 May 2003: 12.

* * * * * * *

JOAQUÍN MORALES

Unlike the majority of Latin American poets, Joaquín Morales, pseudonym of Lito Pessolani (Asunción, 1959-), has worked professionally in a field far removed from literature: Information Technology. He received his formal training at the Universidad Nacional de Asunción, and has worked as a software programmer, most recently on a neural network project. He was an early member of the literary group known as the Taller de Poesía Manuel Ortiz Guerrero in the 1980s. In spite of the fact that Morales does not consider himself a poet, but a dilettante, he has nevertheless received awards and recognitions for his published works: from the Instituto Paraguayo de Cultura Hispánica in 1983; the Instituto Cultural Paraguayo Alemán in 1983; Concurso de Guiones de Radioteatro, Westdeutscher, Rundfunk, 1990; Centro Cultural de la Ciudad de Asunción in 1991; second prize in the "Premio V Centenario de Poesía, 1990;" and first prize for a short story in the "Premio V Centenario de Cuento, 1992." He is a life-long resident of Asunción.

POETRY:

Postales de Bizancio. Asunción: G.A.R., 1984.

Various authors. *Poesía itinerante*. Asunción: Taller, 1984.

Poliedro. Asunción: Alcándara, 1985.

sermo. Asunción: Cuadernos de la Ura, 2005.

musica ficta semitonia subintellecta. Asunción: Jakembo, 2005.

Hurras a Bizancio. Asunción: Jakembo, 2005.

CRITICISM, REVIEWS, INTERVIEWS

Guerrero, Gustavo, ed. *Cuerpo plural. Antología de la poesía hispanoamericana contemporánea*. Madrid-Buenos Aires-Valencia: Instituto Cervantes/Pre-Textos, 2010. Also, see: http://www.poesiadigital.es/index.php?cmd=entrevista&id=65

Haladyna, Ronald. "Un buzón lleno de sorpresas: *Postales de Bizancio* de Joaquín Morales." *Cultural* (*La Nación*) 14 Sept. 1997, 2-3.

---. "Los dos extremos de la poesía paraguaya contemporánea: Carlos Villagra Marsal y Joaquín Morales." *América Sin Nombre: Boletín de la Unidad de Investigación de la Universidad de Alicante* (Alicante, Spain.) ISSN 1577-3442. 4 (2002): 35-41.

Peiró Barco, José Vicente. "*Historias de Babel* de Joaquín Morales: Una radiografía distinta de la dictadura de Stroessner." *Cultural* (*La Nación*) 7 Sept. 2003: 1-2

---. *La narrativa paraguaya actual 1980-1995*. Asunción: Universidad del Norte, 2006. See an extract online at: <http://www.cervantesvirtual.com/FichaObra.html?Ref=6999&text=pdf>

* * * * * * *

AMANDA PEDROZO

Amanda Pedrozo (Asunción, 1955-), an early member of the Taller de Poesía Manuel Ortiz Guerrero, was graduated with a law degree from the University of Asunción. Even before publishing her first book, she was awarded the "Amigos del Arte" first prize in the category of poets under the age of twenty-five in 1984. Although she has published only two books of poetry, her poems have appeared in a number of well-known anthologies: *Y ahora la palabra* (1979); *Poesía Taller* (1982); and *Poesía Itinerante* (1984); *El monte de las delicias* (1993); and *Y vamos haciendo camino* (1993). In addition to her published books of poetry, she has collaborated on two books of short stories: *Mujeres al teléfono y otros cuentos* (1997) with her sister, Mabel; and *Prostibularias* (2003) with Alejandro Maciel and Luis Hernáez. Her short stories and poems have been included in various anthologies, such as *Poetisas del Paraguay* (1992), and more recently she has been contributing to many online virtual anthologies. She has been a news reporter for several dailies in Asunción, and more recently the news director of *Diario Popular.*

POESÍA

*Las cosas usuales.*Asunción: El Lector, 1985.

Mal de amores. Asunción: Arandurã, 2002.

CRITICISM, REVIEWS, INTERVIEWS

Acosta, Delfina. "*Mal de amores* de Amanda Pedrozo." *ABC Color, Suplemento Cultural,* 7 July 2002: 4.

Pla, Josefina. Prólogo. *Las cosas usuales.* By Amanda Pedrozo. Asunción: El Lector, 1985.

Peiró Barco, José Vicente. "La esencia del amor: Amanda Pedrozo." *Mal de Amores.*

Asunción: Arandurã, 2002. 7-13. Reprinted: *Cultural* (*La Nación*) 28 April, 2002: 4-5.

* * * * * * *

JACOBO RAUSKIN

Jacobo Rauskin (Villarica, Paraguay, 1941-) spent his childhood in Villarica and Asunción, but when he was seventeen years old, he was obliged to spend two years in Buenos Aires, seeking refuge from the repression of the Strössner regime. He later returned to Paraguay to study literature, without obtaining a degree, at the Universidad Nacional de Asunción, and afterwards at the University of Texas at Austin and the University of Delaware in Newark. Over the years he has worked as an employee of a cotton company, an insurance representative, a translator, a language teacher, and a news reporter. He has been an advisor for the Municipal Theater of Asunción, and is currently the director of the Biblioteca Municipal Augusto Roa Bastos in Asunción.

In addition to being Paraguay's most prolific poet for almost 50 years, he has devoted his life to his love of literature and especially of poetry: he receives numerous invitations to participate in international poetry festivals; gives frequent poetry readings and workshops in Paraguay; has been a regular contributor to the *Revista Crítica* and literary supplements in Asunción; has taught literature at the Universidad Católica in Asunción; has translated poetry from English, French and Guaraní to Spanish; has edited anthologies of Paraguayan poetry; is a member of the Paraguayan Academy of the Spanish Language and a corresponding member of the Real Academia Española. His renown has grown in recent years, especially since 2007, when he received Paraguay's National Literary Award. He resides in Asunción with his wife Helena.

POETRY

Oda. Asunción: Asunción: Péndulo, 1964.

Linceo. Asunción: Péndulo, 1965.

Casa perdida. Asunción: Fondo Editor Paraguayo, 1971.

Naufragios. Asunción: Alcándara, 1984.

Jardín de la pereza. Asunción: Alcándara, 1987.

La noche del viaje. Tres idilios. Asunción: Loma Clavel, 1988. (Premio La República, 1989.)

La canción andariega. Asunción: Loma Clavel, 1991, (Premio El Lector, 1991.)

Alegría de un hombre que vuelve. Asunción: Loma Clavel, 1992.

Fogata y dormidero de caminantes. Asunción: Arandurã, 1994, (Premio El Lector, 1994); Premio Municipal de Literatura, Asunción, 1996.)

(With other authors.) *Muestra de poesía*. Asunción: Arandurã; Montevideo: La Banda Oriental, 1995. 57-68.

La calle del violín allá lejos. Asunción: Arandurã, 1996.

Adiós a la cigarra. Asunción: Arandurã, 1997. (Premio Roque Gaona de la Sociedad de Escritores del Paraguay, 1997.)

Canciones elegidas (Anthology). Buenos Aires: Tierra Firme, 1998.

Pitogüé. Asunción: Arandurã, 1999.

Poesía 1991-1999. Asunción: Arandurã, 2000. Also, see: <http://www.cervantesvirtual.com/FichaAutor.html?Ref=4131&portal=177)>

La ruta de los pájaros. Asunción: Arandurã, 2000. (Also see: <http://www.cervantesvirtual.com/FichaAutor.html?Ref=4131&portal=177>

Poemas viejos. Asunción: Arandurã, 2001. (Includes selections from *Casa perdida*, *Naufragios*, and complete texts of *Jardín de la pereza* and *La noche del viaje*.)

Andamio para distraídos. Asunción: Arandurã, 2001.

El dibujante callejero. Asunción: Arandurã, 2002.

Doña Ilusión. Asunción: Arandurã, 2003. (Premio Roque Gaona de la Sociedad de Escritores del Paraguay, 2003.)

Poesía reunida. Asunción: Arandurã, 2004. (Includes *Poemas viejos*, *Poesía 1991-1999*, books published between 2001-2003, and a series of unpublished poems entitled *El ciervo herido y otros poemas*, 2004). 2nd ed. Asunción: Arandurã, 2009. (Includes complete text of the 1st ed., as well as *La rebelión demorada*, *Espantadiablos*, and *Los años en el viento*.)

La rebelión demorada. Asunción: Arandurã, 2005.

Los años en el viento. Asunción: Arandurã, 2007.

Espantadiablos. Asunción: Arandurã, 2006. (Premio Nacional de Literatura 2007.) 2nd ed. Asunción: Arandurã, 2008.

Un día pasa un pájaro y otros poemas (Anthology). Arandurã, 2008. (Includes CD with recordings of author reading selected poems.)

Las manos vacías. Asunción: Arandurã, 2010.

La nave. (Anthology). Buenos Aires: Ediciones del Dock, 2010.

CRITICISM, REVIEWS, INTERVIEWS

Acevedo, Hugo. Rev. of *La calle del violín allá lejos*, by Jacobo Rauskin. *La República* (Montevideo) 15 June 1997.

Acosta, Delfina. Rev. of *Adiós a la cigarra*, by Jacobo Rauskin. *ABC Color* 25 July 1997.

---. "Siguiendo *La ruta de los pájaros*, by Jacobo Rauskin." *Suplemento Cultural* (*ABC Color*) 22 Oct. 2000: 2-3.

---. Rev. of *Andamio para distraídos*, by Jacobo Rauskin. *ABC Color* 7 Oct 2001.

---. Rev. of *El dibujante callejero*, by Jacobo Rauskin. *Suplemento Cultural* (*ABC Color)* 22 Sept. 2002: 4.

---. Rev. of *La rebelión demorada*, by Jacobo Rauskin. *ABC*, 17 Apr. 2005.

Appleyard, José-Luis. Rev. of *Casa perdida*, by Jacobo Rauskin. *La Tribuna* Dec 1971.

Benavides, Washington. "Sobre la poesía de Jacobo A. Rauskin." *Exégesis* (Humacao, Puerto Rico) 26 (1996): 34-35. Reprinted: *Litterae* (U of Concepción, Chile): <http://www.litterae.cl/amelia.html>

---. "Algunos datos sobre la poesía de J. A. Rauskin." *Cultural* (*La Nación*): 7 Dec. 1997: 7.

Caballero Aquino, Ricardo. "Rauskin, el viajero." *Noticias*. 18 Nov 1988.

Camerón, Juan. "Rauskin obtiene Premio Nacional de Literatura en Paraguay: *Poesía para espantar diablos*." <http://us.f532.mail.yahoo.com/ym/ShowLetter?Search=&Idx=8&YY=10085&y_5beta=yes&y5beta=yes&order=down&sort=date&pos=0&view=a&head=b>

Casartelli, Mario. "El violín de una constancia." Última Hora n.d. 1996.

Casartelli, Victor. "Jacobo Rauskin." *Arquitrave* Oct. 2008. <http://www.arquitrave.com/archivo_revista/Revista39/rauskin-victor-casartelli.pdf>

---. Cantar las horas perdidas. *Revista de Poesía La Otra* (México City) July-Sept., 2011.l

Chaves, Raquel. Rev. of *Naufragios*, by J.A. Rauskin. *Última Hora* n.d. 1984.

Cutler, Bruce. "Five poems by J.A. Rauskin." *Texas Quarterly* 18.3 (1976).

---. "Encounters" and "Lady, I don't want to be." Trans. and notes by Bruce Cutler. *Nimrod. Latin American Voices.* (University of Tulsa) 18.1 (1973).

De Pablo, Óscar. "Jacobo Rauskin, de pie frente al lenguaje." *Takuapu* (Asunción) Feb. 2007: 8-9.

Delgado, Susy. "Jacobo Rauskin, el poeta que siempre está empezando." *Cultural* (*La Nación*) 24 May 1998: 3-5.

---. "Jacobo Rauskin y la poesía periférica de hoy." *Cultural* (*La Nación*) 1 Apr. 2001: 4-5.

Fernandes, Carla. "Entre tradición y modernidad: la poesía de Jacobo A. Rauskin." *Hispanorama* (Nuremberg, RFA) Nov. 2002: 21-26.

Folguera, Juan José. "Poemas viejos de Jacobo A. Rauskin: Un poeta íntimo vuelve sobre sus pasos." *Cultural* (*La Nación*.) 29 July, 2001: 2-3.

Garat, Alicia. "La poesía no sabe de fronteras." *Crónicas* (Montevideo) 1 Dec. 1995.

González Real, Osvaldo. Rev. of *La noche del viaje*, by Jacobo Rauskin. *Hoy* Dec. 1988.

Haladyna, Ronald. "Quedando a flote con *Naufragios* de Jacobo Rauskin." *Cultural La Nación*) 27 July 1997: 2; 7.

---. "Una pereza bien productiva: *El jardín de la pereza*." *Cultural* (*La Nación*) 3 Aug. 1997: 2; 7.

---. "El goce de lo cotidiana en la poesía de Jacobo A. Rauskin." *J.A. Rauskin: Poesía 1991-1999*. Asunción: Arandurã, 2000. 143-152. Reprinted in *Litterae* (U of Concepción, Chile) April-May 2009: <http://www.litterae.cl/corcuera.html>

--- " Un reconocimiento tardío: La poesía de Jacobo Rauskin" *Revista Posdata*, (Monterrey, México) Jan. 2010.

Hempel B, Carlo W. "Lenguaje poético de Jacobo A. Rauskin." *Noticias* 25 Nov. 1997.

Livieres Banks, Lorenzo. "La obra poética de Jacobo A. Rauskin." *Crítica* (Asunción) 12 (Dec. 1996).

Marini Palmieri, Enrique. "Jacobo Rauskin y la poesía del desencanto." *Takuapu* (Asunción) Dec. 2007: 10-11.

Peiró, José Vicente. "Edificio de la realidad." Rev. of *Andamio para distraídos*, by Jacobo Rauskin. *Correo Semanal* (*Última Hora*) 15-16 Sept. 2001: 18-19.

---. "Elvio Romero, Rubén Bareiro Saguier, Renée Ferrer, Jacobo Rauskin. Calas de la poesía paraguaya." *Dos orillas y un encuentro: La literatura paraguaya actual*. Ed. Mar Langa Pizarro. Alicante, Spain: Universidad de Alicante, 2006. 193-210.

---. "La voz de una personalidad poética." *Litterae* (Universidad de Concepción, Chile) May 2009: <http://www.litterae.cl/tito.html>

---. " Jacobo Rauskin y su poesía del escepticismo." *Revista de Poesía La Otra* (México City) July-Sept. 2010.

Rauskin, Jacobo. "Aquí se invierte en sueldos de burócratas." Interview with Victorio Suárez V. *Literatura paraguaya (1900-2000)*. By Victorio Suárez V. Asunción: Servilibro, 2001. 307-310.

Salas, Horacio. "Sobre la poesía de Jacobo A. Rauskin." *Correo Semanal* (*Última Hora*) 19 Apr. 1997.

Valdés, Edgar. "La poesía de Jacobo A. Rauskin." *Última Hora*. 22 Feb. 1997.

Vallejos, Roque. "Poesía, un paisaje interior." *Última Hora* 8 July 1991.

---. "Rauskin celebra la irrealidad del tiempo." *Última Hora* 12 Sept. 1992.

---. "Alturas de lo lírico-poético." *Última Hora* June 1999.

---. "Difícil facilidad del género poético." *Última Hora* 8 Nov. 2000.

* * * * * * *

ELVIO ROMERO

As a standard bearer for Paraguay's exiled intellectuals before and during the Stroessner dictatorship, Elvio Romero (Yegros, Paraguay, 1926—Buenos Aires, Argentina, 2004) won Paraguay's very first National Prize for Literature for his book, *El poeta y sus circunstancias*. In spite of—or perhaps because of—Romero's leaving in exile from Paraguay during the Revolution of 1947 and returning only occasionally ever since, he is widely considered as Paraguay's most celebrated poet in the last half of the twentieth century. He lived and wrote the majority of his works in Buenos Aires, where the Losada publishing house published and distributed them, and promoted the translation of his poetry into many languages. Before his death in 2004 following a prolonged illness, he was Paraguay's cultural attaché in Buenos Aires.

POETRY

Despiertan las fogatas. Buenos Aires: Losada, 1953.

El sol bajo las raíces. Buenos Aires: Losada, 1956.

De cara al corazón. Buenos Aires: Losada, 1961.

Doce poemas de Elvio Romero. Quito: Casa de la Cultura Ecuatoriana, 1962.

Antología poética: 1947-1964. Buenos Aires: Losada, 1965.

Un relámpago herido: Poesía amorosa (1963-1966.) Buenos Aires: Losada, 1967.

Los innombrables: 1959-1964. Buenos Aires: Losada, 1970.

Días roturados: poemas de la guerra civil. Buenos Aires: Losada, 1972.

Antología poética: 1947-1977. 3rd ed. Buenos Aires: Losada, 1981.

El sol bajo las raíces: 1952-55. [2nd. ed., corrected]. Asunción: Alcándara, 1984.

Los valles imaginarios. Buenos Aires: Losada, 1984.

Despiertan las fogatas … 1950-1952. [Ed. corrected and modified.] Asunción: Alcándara, 1986.

Resoles áridos: 1948-1949. [Corrected ed. with an additional unedited poem.] Asunción: Alcándara, 1987.

Poesías completas. 2 vols. Asunción: Alcántara, 1990.

Elvio Romero: Sus mejores poemas. Asunción: El Lector, 1996.

Antología personal. Buenos Aires: Desde la Gente; Inst. Movilizador de Fondos Cooperativos, 2000.

De cara al corazón: Antología de la poesía amorosa. Asunción: El Lector, 2002.

Contra la vida quieta: Antología / Elvio Romero. Eds. Olga Martínez, José Vicente Peiró and Francisco Robles. Canet de Mar, Spain: Candaya, 2003.

CRITICISM, REVIEWS, INTERVIEWS

Acosta, Delfina. "Para Elvio Romero, la poesía es una vuelta a la desnudez primera." *Suplemento Cultural* (*ABC Color*) 11 May 2003: 4.

Almada Roche, Armando. *La palabra, primer territorio libre de América: Escritores latinoamericanos.* Asunción: Universidad Nacional de Formosa, 1997. 110-113.

---. "Los mejores poemas de Elvio Romero." *Suplemento Cultural* (*ABC Color*) 25 Oct. 1998: 3.

---. "Elvio Romero. El furor del relámpago." *Digital ABC* (Asunción) 22 May 2007: http://www.abc.com.py/especiales/elvio/articulos.php?pid=330931

Asturias, Miguel Angel. Introducción. *El sol bajo las raíces: 1952-55*. By Elvio Romero. 2nd. ed. Asunción: Alcándara, 1984.

Delgado, Susy. "Elvio Romero y las ventanas abiertas." *Cultural* (*La Nación*): 29 Oct. 1995. 2-3.

Domínguez, Ramiro. "El hombre paraguayo en 3 poetas sociales: C. Cervera, Roa Bastoa y Elvio Romero." *Alcor* (Asunción) 16 (1962): 2; 11.

Haladyna, Ronald. "*Los valles imaginarios* de Elvio Romero." *Cultural* (*La Nación*) 7 Dic. 1997. 2-3.

Pecci, Antonio. "Un galardón nacional para Elvio Romero." *Correo Semanal* (*Última Hora*) 24-25 Nov. 2001: 18-19.

Peiró, José Vicente. Prólogo. *Contra la vida quieta: Antología / Elvio Romero*. Eds. Olga Martínez, José Vicente Peiró and Francisco Robles. Canet de Mar, Spain: Candaya, 2003.

---. "Elvio Romero, Rubén Bareiro Saguier, Renée Ferrer, Jacobo Rauskin. Calas de la poesía paraguaya." *Dos orillas y un encuentro: La literatura paraguaya actual*. Ed. Mar Langa Pizarro. Alicante, Spain: Universidad de Alicante, 2006. 193-210.

Plá, Josefina. Prólogo. *Elvio Romero: Sus mejores poemas*. By Elvio Romero. Asunción: El Lector, 1996.

Romero, Elvio. "El neoliberalismo fomenta las diferencias sociales." Interview with Victorio Suárez V. *Literatura paraguaya (1900-2000)*. By Victorio Suárez V. Asunción: Servilibro, 2001. 206-207; 243-249.

Rubio, Ricardo. *Elvio Romero, la fuerza de la realidad*. Asunción: Servilibro, 2003.

Szanto, Endre Fulei. "Realidad e ilusión en los poemas de Elvio Romero." *Horanyi Matyas. Actas del simposio internacional de estudios hispánicos*. Budapest: 18-19 Aug. 1976; Budapest: Akad. Kiado, 1978.

Zubizarreta, Gonzalo. Epílogo. *El sol bajo las raíces: 1952-55*. By Elvio Romero, 2nd. ed. Asunción: Alcándara, 1984.

For a variety links to homages and perspectives on Romero's life and impact as a writer, see: <http://www.sololiteratura.com/elvio/elvionoticiasfall.htm>

* * * * * * *

RICARDO DE LA VEGA

Ricardo de la Vega (Mendoza, Argentina, 1956 -) has resided in Asunción since 1976 and later became a Paraguayan citizen. He was a member of the literary group "Promoción del 80"; a founding member of the Society of Paraguayan Writers (SEP); co-founder of the literary review *Cabichu'í 2*; and founder, director, and editor of the literary review (still in operation) *Revista de Poesía Tren Rojo*. This review sponsored the recent publication of an anthology of Paraguayan poet Esteban Cabañas. In addition, he is a frequent contributor to *Barataria*, a Buenos Aires review devoted to poetry, and together with poets Aurelio González Canale and Genaro Riera, produced a CD "Tres poetas callejeros" [Three Street Poets]. They recite their poems in public venues such as in plazas, markets, and taxi stands in an attempt to spread the contagion of popular poetry.

Among his literary awards are honorable mentions for the Concurso Poesía Joven del Instituto de Cultura Hispánica (1980, 1983) and the Instituto Paraguayo-Alemán (1983); second prizes in competitions in the Instituto de Cultura Hispana (1985); first prize from the Academia de Ex-Alumnos del San José (2003); and an honorable mention from the Juan S. Netto poetry competition (2008.) Vega has also established himself as an author of short stories, winning awards in 1995, 2003, and 2007. He has been a traveling pharmaceutical and medical equipment salesman for the past thirty years.

POETRY

Sin opciones después de la cena. Asunción: Taller, 1985.

Notable paraíso. Asunción: Diálogo, 1995.

La canción de R. Asunción: Arandurã, 1999.

Afuera. Asunción: Arandurã, 2002.

Cincuenta y cuatro, poesía. Asunción: Arandurã, 2003.

Canto al Mariscal Francisco Solano López. Asunción: Arandurã, 2006.

Cuídame el corazón. Pending publication in 2011.

CRITICISM, REVIEWS, INTERVIEWS

Acosta, Delfina. "'Los hombres ya no invitan a cenar' de Ricardo de la Vega." *Suplemento Cultural* (*ABC Color*) 17 June 2001, 2-3.

---. "*Afuera*, un libro polémico de Ricardo de la Vega." *Suplemento Cultural* (*ABC Color*) 19 Jan 2003: 4.

---. "Ricardo de la Vega y su nuevo poemario [*Afuera*]." *Suplemento Cultural ABC Color* 23 June 2002: 4.

Delgado, Susy. Rev. of *Afuera*, by Ricardo de la Vega. *Cultural* (*La Nación*) 29 Dec. 2002: 8.

Haladyna, Ronald. "Opciones poéticas de Ricardo de la Vega." *Cultural* (*La Nación*) 9 Nov. 1997: 2-3.

Martínez, Luis María. Prólogo. *La canción de R*. By Ricardo de la Vega. Asunción: Arandurã, 1999.

Peiro, José Vicente. "Ricardo de la Vega." *Cultural* (*La Nación*) 30 May 2003: 4.

Rauskin, J.A. "Sobre la poesía que vive en este libro." *La canción de R.* By Ricardo de la Vega. Asunción: Arandurã, 1999.

Rodríguez Alcalá, Hugo. "El primer libro de poemas de Ricardo de la Vega: *Sin opciones después de la cena.*" *Diario Noticias* (Asunción) 1995.

Ruiz Nesterosa, Jesús. "Las dos vertientes de Ricardo de la Vega." Rev. of *Notable Paraíso.* By Ricardo de la Vega. *Suplemento Cultural (ABC Color*) 29 Oct. 1995: 2-3.

Vallory, María José. "Belleza que surge desde lo sórdido." *Última Hora* 8 June 2001: 32.

Vallejos, Roque. "Las calas del amor profundo." *Última Hora* (Asunción) 1999.

Vega, Ricardo de la. Interview with Victorio Suárez V. *Las voces más importantes de la literatura paraguaya.* By Victorio Suárez V. Asunción: Servilibro, 2001.

---. "Me da pena la claudicación de muchos poetas." Interview with Victorio Suárez V. *Literatura paraguaya (1900-2000).* By Victorio Suárez V. Asunción: Servilibro, 2001. 399-402.

* * * * * * *

CARLOS VILLAGRA MARSAL

Born and reared in Asunción, Carlos Villagra Marsal (1932-) began writing early and soon became a member of a notable literary group of writers—la Promoción del 50—that started publishing in the 1950s. He concluded his studies in law, but also received his Bachelor's degree in Philosophy and Letters at the Universidad Nacional de Asunción, and did postgraduate studies at the Universidad Central in Madrid, and the Sorbonne in Paris. He traveled abroad extensively for years, resided in Spain and France, while being active as a poet, narrator, newsman, essayist, researcher, culinary anthropologist, and especially as a professor (in Ecuador, France, and Spain.) For many years he was director of the

Tertulia Literaria Hispanoamericana de Asunción, a literary guild devoted to discussing and promoting literature in Spanish American countries.

Among other activities, he has been a professor of Guaraní literature at the Universidad Católica and the Universidad Nacional, both in Asunción, an editor of the Araverá Press in Asunción from 1985 to 1987, and is perhaps best known as co-founder and director of the Alcándara Press, which published over sixty works of Paraguayan poets in the six years of his tenure (1982-1988.) He was elected to the Paraguayan Academy of the Language and is a correspondent of the Real Academia Española.

Villagra served as Paraguay's ambassador in Chile (1997-99) and in Ecuador (1999-2003.) His one book of narrative literature—*Mancuello y la peredíz* (1965)—won an award in 1965 from *La Tribuna* (Asunción) for best novel; it has been republished many times in Asunción and abroad. His poetic production is not prolific, but important: poems of his have been included in *Poésie paraguayenne du XXe siècle d'expression espagnole*, and he has received various literary awards. He currently resides in Asunción and is professor of literature and linguistics at the Universidad Nacional de Asunción, and conducts a radio program on Paraguayan culture.

POETRY

Antología mínima. Asunción: Author's ed., 1975.

Guarania del desvelado: 1954-1979. Buenos Aires: Losada, 1979.

El júbilo difícil (Poesía 1986-1995.) Ed. Raúl Amaral. Asunción: Don Bosco, 1995.

Variaciones en dos claves. Poesías. /El júbilo difícil (Poesía 1986-1995). Ed. Raúl Amaral. Asunción: Don Bosco, 1995.

Poesía congregada y otros afanes. Asunción: Servilibros, 2007.

CRITICISM, REVIEWS, INTERVIEWS

Acosta, Delfina. "Erudición en la poesía de Carlos Villagra Marsal." *Suplemento Cultural*, (*ABC Color*) 2 March 2003: 4.

Amaral, Raúl. "La poesía natural y profunda de Carlos Villagra Marsal." *El júbilo difícil: Poesía 1986-1995*. By Carlos Villagra Marsal. Asunción: Don Bosco, 1995.

Delgado, Susy. "Carlos Villagra Marsal, el júbilo de vivir." *Cultural* (*La Nación*) 22 Oct. 1995: 2-3.

Haladyna, Ronald. "*El júbilo difícil* de Villagra Marsal." *Cultural* (*La Nación*) 7 Dec. 1997, 2-3.

Rodríguez-Alcalá, Hugo. "Carlos Villagra Marsal, Desvuelos en la Alcándara." *Poetas y prosistas paraguayos y otros breves ensayos*. Asunción: Intercontinental, 1988. 133-138.

Valdés, Edgar. "La poesía de Carlos Villagra Marsal." *Última Hora* (*Correo Semanal,* 25 Nov. 1995: 8-9.

Villagra Marsal. "Entrevista con Carlos Villagra Marsal." Interview with Juan Manuel Marcos. *Discurso Literario: Revista de Temas Hispánicos* (Stillwater, Oklahoma) 3.2 (1986): 247-261.

---. "Entrevista con Carlos Villagra Marsal." Interview with Michael Moody. *Confluencia: Revista Hispánica de Cultura y Literatura*. 5.1 (1989): 101-107.

---. "Hay capillas aúlicas donde se aplaude el servilismo." Interview with Victorio Suárez V. *Literatura paraguaya (1900-2000)*. By Victorio Suárez V. Asunción: Servilibro, 2001. 273-278.

For additional updated information on the poet and access to some of his poetry, see "Portal Guarani" at http://www.portalguarani.com/autores_detalles.php?id=578

Also, for a selection of the poetry of Carlos Villagra Marsal, see: http://www.festivaldepoesiademedellin.org/pub.php/es/Revista/ultimas_ediciones/86_87/villagra.html

* * * * * * *

ABOUT THE EDITOR

Ronald Haladyna, became professor emeritus of Spanish and Latin American Culture in 2009 after twenty-five years at Ferris State University, Big Rapids, Michigan. His experience in Latin America is varied and extensive: Peace Corps Volunteer (1967-1969) in Cusco, Peru; professor of English at the Universidad Autónoma del Estado de México (Toluca, Mexico 1974-1984); senior Fulbright lecturer and researcher in Asunción, Paraguay (1997); and researcher with travel grants and sabbatical leaves in South America (1997-2008). Author of ***The Tourism Industry: Readings in English*** (1992), ***Rescatando la poesía paraguaya: Diez ensayos sobre nueve poetas*** (1998), ***La poesía postmoderna mexicana: Pedro Salvador Ale, David Huerta y Coral Bracho*** (1999), co-translator of Renée Ferrer's ***Sobreviviente/Survivor*** (1999), and editor of ***Contemporary Uruguayan Poetry: A Bilingual Anthology.*** Dr. Haladyna is currently preparing anthologies on other contemporary South American poetry. He resides on a nature preserve near Big Rapids, Michigan.